luke

D0034058

the gospel according to

luke

authorised king james version

printed by authority

published by canongate

---

with an introduction by | richard holloway

First published in Great Britain in 1998
by Canongate Books Ltd
14 High Street, Edinburgh EH1 1TE

10 9 8 7 6 5 4 3 2

Introduction copyright © Richard Holloway 1998
The moral right of the author has been asserted

British Library Cataloguing-in-Publication Data
A catalogue record is available on request from
the British Library

ISBN 0 86241 797 X

Typeset by Palimpsest Book Production
Book design by Paddy Cramsie
Printed and bound in Great Britain
by Caledonian International, Bishopbriggs

a note about pocket canons

The Authorised King James Version of the Bible, translated between 1603–11, coincided with an extraordinary flowering of English literature. This version, more than any other, and possibly more than any other work in history, has had an influence in shaping the language we speak and write today. Presenting individual books from the Bible as separate volumes, as they were originally conceived, encourages the reader to approach them as literary works in their own right.

The first twelve books in this series encompass categories as diverse as history, fiction, philosophy, love poetry and law. Each Pocket Canon also has its own introduction, specially commissioned from an impressive range of writers, which provides a personal interpretation of the text and explores its contemporary relevance.

Richard Holloway was born in Glasgow in 1933. He is a well-known writer and broadcaster. His last book, Dancing on the Edge, *was published by Harper Collins in 1997. He has been Bishop of Edinburgh since 1986, and Gresham Professor of Divinity in London since 1997.*

introduction by richard holloway

There is a lot to be said for attaching a health warning to religion. It can be a hazardous business, because it is often based on a seductive deceit. In its most dangerous form it claims to have found words that exactly express one of the great mysteries that obsess the imagination, the possibility of God. So words *about* God are treated as though they were equivalent to God, and religious authorities demand our assent to them. Our fidelity or infidelity is tested by our relationship to the official vocabulary that is supposed to express the divine mystery. Since there is no final way of either verifying or falsifying such claims, the opportunity religious language offers us for violence and discord is endless. This is why many of the sanest minds in history have been wary of religion and its explosive, but unsustainable claims.

Apart from the danger religion may pose to our physical health, it can also endanger us spiritually, because it can trap us in language *about* mysteries rather than open us to the mysteries themselves. One of our problems as humans is that our greatest gift, language, is also our greatest danger. We destroy ourselves by our words. The difficulty is that things are not what we say they are. The word 'water' is not itself drinkable. Words point to things, but they can never be the things they point to. This may seem too obvious to waste time on, but it is a truth that is often ignored in religious circles. All theology is a doomed but necessary attempt to express the inexpressible. God is the elusive mystery we try to capture and convey in language, but how can that ever be done? If the word 'water' is not itself drinkable, how can the words we use to express the mystery of God be themselves absolute? They are metaphors, analogies, figures of speech, yet religious people have slaughtered and condemned each other over these experimental uncertainties. Our glory and agony is that we long to find words that will no longer be words, mere signifiers, but the very experience they are trying to signify; and our tragedy is that we can never succeed. This is the anguish that lies at the heart of all religion, because, though our words can describe our thirst for the absolute, they can never satisfy it.

But there is something that comes close. There is a human experience that sometimes captures the mystery that haunts us. Music is usually held to be the experience that does this best. In music there is an almost perfect equivalence of form and content. Music evidences itself, is itself the experience we experience, and is not just a sign or symbol for something else. All great art does this. It breaks through the frustration of language and unites us with that which words only usually signify. I say, 'only usually', because there is a language that, like music and art, is also capable of this same perfect tautology, this mysterious equivalence between the longing and the thing longed for. I am, of course, talking about poetry. Art, particularly music and poetry, unites us with the thing beyond, places us in its midst, rather than talks unceasingly and ineffectively about it, which is what religion usually does.

One test of great art is the shiver factor, the prickle at the back of the neck, the involuntary twitch of muscle that shows that a connection has been made between us and the matter to which we are paying attention. By this standard, Luke's gospel is a work of great art. In place after place it achieves that mysterious equivalence between the word spoken and the word felt, the situation described and the situation experienced. This is why it has influenced other artists who have translated Luke's words into painting of equivalent power. One of these paintings hangs in the Royal Scottish Gallery in Edinburgh. It was painted by Giovanni Francesco Barbieri for Cardinal Rocci in 1639 and it is called *Peter the Penitent*. It shows Peter crying bitterly, tormented by anguish and guilt, just after his third denial of Jesus. All the gospels recount the prediction of Jesus that Peter would deny him, and they all go on to describe Peter's betrayal. Only in *Luke*, however, do we get the detail that makes dramatic sense of Peter's desolation. After the third denial the cock crows, and Luke tells us: 'And the Lord turned, and looked upon Peter. And Peter remembered the word of the Lord, how he had said unto him, "Before the cock crow, thou shalt deny me thrice." And Peter went out, and wept bitterly' (22:61–2). The words are few and simple, yet they have carried that look of grieving love through history. And they connect us to our own denials. Peter's tragedy is not that he was a bad or cynical man, but that he was an ordinary man who could not live up to his own ideals. Luke does not use abstract language about human remorse and the nature of guilt, yet in a few brush-strokes he brings us right into the experience and we confront ourselves. Unlike much conventional religious teaching that alienates us by its hectoring abstractions, Luke connects with us again and again by the immediacy of his art.

But that way of putting it is misleading, because it suggests the self-conscious presence of a writer working away to put a perfect polish on the text. We do not know who Luke was, and it does not matter, because it is the very anonymity of this text that confirms its power. All great art is essentially anonymous in its impact. We do not need to know anything about its provenance for it to affect us. We do not really know who wrote *Genesis* or many of the other ancient writings and we need not care, because these great texts communicate truth to us at a level that goes beyond the artistry of any particular individual. They create archetypes that express the general condition of humanity, and its sorrow and loss, heroism and betrayal. This is also why the gospels go on touching us long after we have abandoned the orthodoxies that have been built on them. We do not know who wrote them or when, but they still have power to connect with our lives today, so that, reading them, we sometimes have to put them down and look into the distance as their words strike ancient chords within us.

If we fed the four gospels into a computer programmed to do literary detective work, we would make some interesting discoveries. The first thing we would notice is that *John*, the fourth gospel, is unlike the other three in voice and perspective. There are differences among the first three gospels as well, of course, but not only do they have a similar feel, they actually share a lot of material. For instance, it is quite obvious that *Matthew* and *Luke* simply repeat large chunks of *Mark*; they each quote another another source, not found in *Mark*; and there is a certain amount of material peculiar to each of them. And all these layers of text had their own history. The gospels were not written down the way a biographer would work today. The process would be more like that of a musical historian who goes round the highlands and islands of Scotland to record folk tales, poetry and songs that are in the memories of people, but have never been written down in hard form. Most of our ancient literature comes from a long-standing oral tradition before it was committed to ink on parchment. The gospel writers would have been engaged in a similar exercise. They would collect stories about Jesus, remembrances that were handed down and sermons or meditations that were the result of long contemplation on the meaning of his story. In time, these would be woven into a whole garment, but only whole in the sense that a patchwork quilt is whole, stitched together out of many pieces.

Some of the most attractive and colourful of the patches are found only in *Luke*. It is Luke who tells us that at his birth Jesus was laid in a manger, 'because there was no room for them in the inn'. Luke brings more women, and more details about them, into his narrative than any of the other gospel writers. We have already noted the little thread of narrative that frames Peter's grief at his denials of Jesus; even more vivid are the parables that have gone into the memory and vocabulary of the western world, such as the Good Samaritan and the Prodigal Son. The message of Jesus, the good news,

richard holloway   xi or gospel, as it was called, was expressed most memorably in the immediacy of stories rather than in religious abstractions. This is why the parables in *Luke* continue to connect with us today. They are about our experience of guilt, and our need for forgiveness; they are about the dangers of tribe and religion, and the way they insulate us against the needs of our neighbours. This is the point of the parable of the Good Samaritan in chapter 10. It is not about religious hypocrisy, and the way religion often says one thing and does another. The reason why the priest and the Levite passed by on the other side, leaving the man lying by the roadside, is that their code would not allow them to come to the aid of a stranger who might be a source of religious pollution to them. Interestingly, the Samaritan also followed a code that was just as defensive towards strangers, but it was simply blown away by the force of the pity he felt for the man who had fallen among thieves. Jesus is warning us that the codes that define our religious and national identities can shut our hearts against one another. Compassion should overrule code.

The story of the Prodigal Son in chapter 15 is even more profound. It is about the ways we hurt one another, and withhold the forgiveness that alone can heal the wounds we have inflicted. The most difficult of the predicaments that face us is what to do about the evil we do to one another. Our pain at being injured, as well as our sense of justice, require confession and repentance from the offender. Being the offender is even more imprisoning. The complexity of guilty self-knowledge often leads to a blustering defensiveness, rather like Peter's denials of Jesus, that prevents us from asking for the forgiveness we desperately want. In this way a dynamic of mutual recrimination is created that traps us in anger and despair. In the parable of the Prodigal the father rushes to forgive the son before he can say a word: 'When he was yet a great way off, his father saw him, and had compassion, and ran, and fell on his neck, and kissed him'. And it is this act of compassionate forgiveness that frees the son from the burden of his own guilt and gives him the strength to confess it: 'Father, I have sinned against heaven, and in thy sight, and am no more worthy to be called thy son'. Jesus is not discussing the ethics of forgiveness, how we can earn it and under what circumstances we can offer it. He simply shows us that without it we are all in prison, so we should try to get our forgiveness in first. If we refuse to forgive, we tear down the very bridge we ourselves will one day have to cross.

The Gospel of Luke is an old book and there is much in it that will seem strange to someone picking it up for the first time today. Nevertheless, it is impossible to read it without being challenged by the mysterious presence of Jesus. As well as a sense of enormous compassion for the human condition, we find in him a burning anger against all systems, religious or political, that come between God and the poor of the earth. In the furious pity of Jesus we catch a glimpse of God's dream for a transformed humanity. But the long narrative of the crucifixion at the end of the gospel reminds us that dreamers are usually disposed of with cruel efficiency by the people who have put themselves in charge of the world. Yet Jesus keeps breaking out of the tombs into which we have consigned him, so the dream lives on.

richard holloway   xiii

the gospel according to st luke

Forasmuch as many have taken in hand to set forth in order
a declaration of those things which are most surely believed
among us, ² even as they delivered them unto us, which from
the beginning were eye-witnesses, and ministers of the word;
³ it seemed good to me also, having had perfect understanding of all things from the very first, to write unto thee in
order, most excellent Theophilus, ⁴ that thou mightest know
the certainty of those things, wherein thou hast been instructed.

⁵ There was in the days of Herod, the king of Judæa, a
certain priest named Zacharias, of the course of Abia; and
his wife was of the daughters of Aaron, and her name was
Elisabeth. ⁶ And they were both righteous before God, walk-
ing in all the commandments and ordinances of the Lord
blameless. ⁷ And they had no child, because that Elisabeth
was barren, and they both were now well stricken in years.

⁸ And it came to pass, that while he executed the priest's
office before God in the order of his course, ⁹ according to the
custom of the priest's office, his lot was to burn incense
when he went into the temple of the Lord. ¹⁰ And the whole
multitude of the people were praying without at the time of
incense. ¹¹ And there appeared unto him an angel of the Lord
standing on the right side of the altar of incense. ¹² And when
Zacharias saw him, he was troubled, and fear fell upon him.
¹³ But the angel said unto him, 'Fear not, Zacharias, for thy

prayer is heard; and thy wife Elisabeth shall bear thee a son, and thou shalt call his name John. [14]And thou shalt have joy and gladness; and many shall rejoice at his birth. [15]For he shall be great in the sight of the Lord, and shall drink neither wine nor strong drink; and he shall be filled with the Holy Ghost, even from his mother's womb. [16]And many of the children of Israel shall he turn to the Lord their God. [17]And he shall go before him in the spirit and power of Elias, to turn the hearts of the fathers to the children, and the disobedient to the wisdom of the just; to make ready a people prepared for the Lord.' [18]And Zacharias said unto the angel, 'Whereby shall I know this? For I am an old man, and my wife well stricken in years.' [19]And the angel answering said unto him, 'I am Gabriel, that stand in the presence of God; and am sent to speak unto thee, and to shew thee these glad tidings. [20]And, behold, thou shalt be dumb, and not able to speak, until the day that these things shall be performed, because thou believest not my words, which shall be fulfilled in their season.'

[21]And the people waited for Zacharias, and marvelled that he tarried so long in the temple. [22]And when he came out, he could not speak unto them; and they perceived that he had seen a vision in the temple, for he beckoned unto them, and remained speechless. [23]And it came to pass, that, as soon as the days of his ministration were accomplished, he departed to his own house.

[24]And after those days his wife Elisabeth conceived, and hid herself five months, saying, [25]'Thus hath the Lord dealt with me in the days wherein he looked on me, to take away my reproach among men.'

²⁶And in the sixth month the angel Gabriel was sent from God unto a city of Galilee, named Nazareth, ²⁷to a virgin espoused to a man whose name was Joseph, of the house of David; and the virgin's name was Mary. ²⁸And the angel came in unto her, and said, 'Hail, thou that art highly favoured, the Lord is with thee: blessed art thou among women.' ²⁹And when she saw him, she was troubled at his saying, and cast in her mind what manner of salutation this should be. ³⁰And the angel said unto her, 'Fear not, Mary, for thou hast found favour with God. ³¹And, behold, thou shalt conceive in thy womb, and bring forth a son, and shalt call his name JESUS. ³² He shall be great, and shall be called the Son of the Highest; and the Lord God shall give unto him the throne of his father David. ³³And he shall reign over the house of Jacob for ever; and of his kingdom there shall be no end.' ³⁴Then said Mary unto the angel, 'How shall this be, seeing I know not a man?' ³⁵And the angel answered and said unto her, 'The Holy Ghost shall come upon thee, and the power of the Highest shall overshadow thee; therefore also that holy thing which shall be born of thee shall be called the Son of God. ³⁶And, behold, thy cousin Elisabeth, she hath also conceived a son in her old age; and this is the sixth month with her, who was called barren. ³⁷ For with God nothing shall be impossible.' ³⁸And Mary said, 'Behold the handmaid of the Lord; be it unto me according to thy word.' And the angel departed from her.

³⁹And Mary arose in those days, and went into the hill country with haste, into a city of Juda; ⁴⁰and entered into the house of Zacharias, and saluted Elisabeth. ⁴¹And it came to pass, that, when Elisabeth heard the salutation of Mary, the babe leaped in her womb; and Elisabeth was filled with the

Holy Ghost. ⁴²And she spake out with a loud voice, and said, 'Blessed art thou among women, and blessed is the fruit of thy womb. ⁴³And whence is this to me, that the mother of my Lord should come to me? ⁴⁴For, lo, as soon as the voice of thy salutation sounded in mine ears, the babe leaped in my womb for joy. ⁴⁵And blessed is she that believed: for there shall be a performance of those things which were told her from the Lord.' ⁴⁶And Mary said,

'My soul doth magnify the Lord,
⁴⁷and my spirit hath rejoiced in God my Saviour.
⁴⁸For he hath regarded the low estate
    of his handmaiden;
        for, behold, from henceforth
    all generations shall call me blessed.
⁴⁹For he that is mighty hath done to me great things;
    and holy is his name.
⁵⁰And his mercy is on them that fear him
    from generation to generation.
⁵¹He hath shewed strength with his arm;
    he hath scattered the proud
        in the imagination of their hearts.
⁵²He hath put down the mighty from their seats,
    and exalted them of low degree.
⁵³He hath filled the hungry with good things;
    and the rich he hath sent empty away.
⁵⁴He hath holpen his servant Israel,
    in remembrance of his mercy;
⁵⁵as he spake to our fathers, to Abraham,
    and to his seed for ever.'

⁵⁶And Mary abode with her about three months, and returned to her own house.

⁵⁷ Now Elisabeth's full time came that she should be delivered; and she brought forth a son. ⁵⁸And her neighbours and her cousins heard how the Lord had shewed great mercy upon her; and they rejoiced with her.

⁵⁹And it came to pass, that on the eighth day they came to circumcise the child; and they called him Zacharias, after the name of his father. ⁶⁰And his mother answered and said, 'Not so; but he shall be called John.' ⁶¹And they said unto her, 'There is none of thy kindred that is called by this name.' ⁶²And they made signs to his father, how he would have him called. ⁶³And he asked for a writing table, and wrote, saying, 'His name is John.' And they marvelled all. ⁶⁴And his mouth was opened immediately, and his tongue loosed, and he spake, and praised God. ⁶⁵And fear came on all that dwelt round about them: and all these sayings were noised abroad throughout all the hill country of Judæa. ⁶⁶And all they that heard them laid them up in their hearts, saying, 'What manner of child shall this be!' And the hand of the Lord was with him.

⁶⁷And his father Zacharias was filled with the Holy Ghost, and prophesied, saying, ⁶⁸ 'Blessed be the Lord God of Israel; for he hath visited and redeemed his people, ⁶⁹ and hath raised up an horn of salvation for us in the house of his servant David, ⁷⁰ as he spake by the mouth of his holy prophets, which have been since the world began, ⁷¹ that we should be saved from our enemies, and from the hand of all that hate us, ⁷² to perform the mercy promised to our fathers, and to remember his holy covenant, ⁷³ the oath which he sware to our father Abraham, ⁷⁴ that he would grant unto us, that we

being delivered out of the hand of our enemies might serve him without fear, [75] in holiness and righteousness before him, all the days of our life. [76]And thou, child, shalt be called the prophet of the Highest; for thou shalt go before the face of the Lord to prepare his ways, [77]to give knowledge of salvation unto his people by the remission of their sins, [78] through the tender mercy of our God; whereby the dayspring from on high hath visited us, [79] to give light to them that sit in darkness and in the shadow of death, to guide our feet into the way of peace.' [80]And the child grew, and waxed strong in spirit, and was in the deserts till the day of his shewing unto Israel.

2 And it came to pass in those days, that there went out a decree from Caesar Augustus, that all the world should be taxed. [2](And this taxing was first made when Cyrenius was governor of Syria.) [3]And all went to be taxed, every one into his own city. [4]And Joseph also went up from Galilee, out of the city of Nazareth, into Judæa, unto the city of David, which is called Bethlehem (because he was of the house and lineage of David), [5] to be taxed with Mary his espoused wife, being great with child. [6]And so it was, that, while they were there, the days were accomplished that she should be delivered. [7]And she brought forth her firstborn son, and wrapped him in swaddling clothes, and laid him in a manger; because there was no room for them in the inn. [8]And there were in the same country shepherds abiding in the field, keeping watch over their flock by night. [9]And, lo, the angel of the Lord came upon them, and the glory of the Lord shone round about them; and they were sore afraid. [10]And the angel said unto them, 'Fear not: for, behold, I bring you good tidings of

great joy, which shall be to all people. ¹¹For unto you is born this day in the city of David a Saviour, which is Christ the Lord. ¹²And this shall be a sign unto you: ye shall find the babe wrapped in swaddling clothes, lying in a manger.' ¹³And suddenly there was with the angel a multitude of the heavenly host praising God, and saying, ¹⁴'Glory to God in the highest, and on earth peace, good will toward men.'

¹⁵And it came to pass, as the angels were gone away from them into heaven, the shepherds said one to another, 'Let us now go even unto Bethlehem, and see this thing which is come to pass, which the Lord hath made known unto us.' ¹⁶And they came with haste, and found Mary, and Joseph, and the babe lying in a manger. ¹⁷And when they had seen it, they made known abroad the saying which was told them concerning this child. ¹⁸And all they that heard it wondered at those things which were told them by the shepherds. ¹⁹But Mary kept all these things, and pondered them in her heart. ²⁰And the shepherds returned, glorifying and praising God for all the things that they had heard and seen, as it was told unto them.

²¹And when eight days were accomplished for the circumcising of the child, his name was called JESUS, which was so named of the angel before he was conceived in the womb.

²²And when the days of her purification according to the law of Moses were accomplished, they brought him to Jerusalem, to present him to the Lord ²³(as it is written in the law of the Lord, 'Every male that openeth the womb shall be called holy to the Lord'), ²⁴and to offer a sacrifice according to that which is said in the law of the Lord, 'a pair of turtledoves, or two young pigeons.' ²⁵And, behold, there was a man

in Jerusalem, whose name was Simeon; and the same man was just and devout, waiting for the consolation of Israel, and the Holy Ghost was upon him. ²⁶And it was revealed unto him by the Holy Ghost that he should not see death before he had seen the Lord's Christ. ²⁷And he came by the Spirit into the temple; and when the parents brought in the child Jesus, to do for him after the custom of the law, ²⁸then took he him up in his arms, and blessed God, and said, ²⁹'Lord, now lettest thou thy servant depart in peace, according to thy word: ³⁰'For mine eyes have seen thy salvation, ³¹which thou hast prepared before the face of all people, ³²a light to lighten the Gentiles, and the glory of thy people Israel.'

³³And Joseph and his mother marvelled at those things which were spoken of him. ³⁴And Simeon blessed them, and said unto Mary his mother, 'Behold, this child is set for the fall and rising again of many in Israel; and for a sign which shall be spoken against ³⁵(yea, a sword shall pierce through thy own soul also), that the thoughts of many hearts may be revealed.'

³⁶And there was one Anna, a prophetess, the daughter of Phanuel, of the tribe of Aser. She was of a great age, and had lived with an husband seven years from her virginity; ³⁷and she was a widow of about fourscore and four years, which departed not from the temple, but served God with fastings and prayers night and day. ³⁸And she coming in that instant gave thanks likewise unto the Lord, and spake of him to all them that looked for redemption in Jerusalem.

³⁹And when they had performed all things according to the law of the Lord, they returned into Galilee, to their own city Nazareth. ⁴⁰And the child grew, and waxed strong in spirit,

filled with wisdom; and the grace of God was upon him.

⁴¹Now his parents went to Jerusalem every year at the feast of the passover. ⁴²And when he was twelve years old, they went up to Jerusalem after the custom of the feast. ⁴³And when they had fulfilled the days, as they returned, the child Jesus tarried behind in Jerusalem; and Joseph and his mother knew not of it. ⁴⁴But they, supposing him to have been in the company, went a day's journey; and they sought him among their kinsfolk and acquaintance. ⁴⁵And when they found him not, they turned back again to Jerusalem, seeking him. ⁴⁶And it came to pass, that after three days they found him in the temple, sitting in the midst of the doctors, both hearing them, and asking them questions. ⁴⁷And all that heard him were astonished at his understanding and answers. ⁴⁸And when they saw him, they were amazed; and his mother said unto him, 'Son, why hast thou thus dealt with us? Behold, thy father and I have sought thee sorrowing.'

⁴⁹And he said unto them, 'How is it that ye sought me? Wist ye not that I must be about my Father's business?' ⁵⁰And they understood not the saying which he spake unto them. ⁵¹And he went down with them, and came to Nazareth, and was subject unto them; but his mother kept all these sayings in her heart.

⁵²And Jesus increased in wisdom and stature, and in favour with God and man.

3 Now in the fifteenth year of the reign of Tiberius Cæsar, Pontius Pilate being governor of Judæa, and Herod being tetrarch of Galilee, and his brother Philip tetrarch of Ituræa and of the region of Trachonitis, and Lysanias the tetrarch of

Abilene, ²Annas and Caiaphas being the high priests, the word of God came unto John the son of Zacharias in the wilderness. ³And he came into all the country about Jordan, preaching the baptism of repentance for the remission of sins; ⁴as it is written in the book of the words of Esaias the prophet, saying, 'The voice of one crying in the wilderness, "Prepare ye the way of the Lord, make his paths straight. ⁵Every valley shall be filled, and every mountain and hill shall be brought low; and the crooked shall be made straight, and the rough ways shall be made smooth; ⁶and all flesh shall see the salvation of God."' ⁷Then said he to the multitude that came forth to be baptized of him, 'O generation of vipers, who hath warned you to flee from the wrath to come? ⁸Bring forth therefore fruits worthy of repentance, and begin not to say within yourselves, "We have Abraham to our father," for I say unto you that God is able of these stones to raise up children unto Abraham. ⁹And now also the axe is laid unto the root of the trees; every tree therefore which bringeth not forth good fruit is hewn down, and cast into the fire.'

¹⁰And the people asked him, saying, 'What shall we do then?' ¹¹He answereth and saith unto them, 'He that hath two coats, let him impart to him that hath none; and he that hath meat, let him do likewise.' ¹²Then came also publicans to be baptized, and said unto him, 'Master, what shall we do?' ¹³And he said unto them, 'Exact no more than that which is appointed you.' ¹⁴And the soldiers likewise demanded of him, saying, 'And what shall we do?' And he said unto them, 'Do violence to no man, neither accuse any falsely; and be content with your wages.'

¹⁵And as the people were in expectation, and all men

mused in their hearts of John, whether he were the Christ, or not, ¹⁶ John answered, saying unto them all, 'I indeed baptize you with water; but one mightier than I cometh, the latchet of whose shoes I am not worthy to unloose; he shall baptize you with the Holy Ghost and with fire, ¹⁷ whose fan is in his hand, and he will throughly purge his floor, and will gather the wheat into his garner; but the chaff he will burn with fire unquenchable.'

¹⁸ And many other things in his exhortation preached he unto the people. ¹⁹ But Herod the tetrarch, being reproved by him for Herodias his brother Philip's wife, and for all the evils which Herod had done, ²⁰ added yet this above all, that he shut up John in prison.

²¹ Now when all the people were baptized, it came to pass, that Jesus also being baptized, and praying, the heaven was opened, ²² and the Holy Ghost descended in a bodily shape like a dove upon him, and a voice came from heaven, which said, 'Thou art my beloved Son; in thee I am well pleased.'

²³ And Jesus himself began to be about thirty years of age, being (as was supposed) the son of Joseph, which was the son of Heli, ²⁴ which was the son of Matthat, which was the son of Levi, which was the son of Melchi, which was the son of Janna, which was the son of Joseph, ²⁵ which was the son of Mattathias, which was the son of Amos, which was the son of Naum, which was the son of Esli, which was the son of Nagge, ²⁶ which was the son of Maath, which was the son of Mattathias, which was the son of Semei, which was the son of Joseph, which was the son of Juda, ²⁷ which was the son of Joanna, which was the son of Rhesa, which was the son of Zorobabel, which was the son of Salathiel, which was the son of Neri,

²⁸ which was the son of Melchi, which was the son of Addi, which was the son of Cosam, which was the son of Elmodam, which was the son of Er, ²⁹ which was the son of Jose, which was the son of Eliezer, which was the son of Jorim, which was the son of Matthat, which was the son of Levi, ³⁰ which was the son of Simeon, which was the son of Juda, which was the son of Joseph, which was the son of Jonan, which was the son of Eliakim, ³¹ which was the son of Melea, which was the son of Menan, which was the son of Mattatha, which was the son of Nathan, which was the son of David, ³² which was the son of Jesse, which was the son of Obed, which was the son of Booz, which was the son of Salmon, which was the son of Naasson, ³³ which was the son of Aminadab, which was the son of Aram, which was the son of Esrom, which was the son of Phares, which was the son of Juda, ³⁴ which was the son of Jacob, which was the son of Isaac, which was the son of Abraham, which was the son of Thara, which was the son of Nachor, ³⁵ which was the son of Saruch, which was the son of Ragau, which was the son of Phalec, which was the son of Heber, which was the son of Sala, ³⁶ which was the son of Cainan, which was the son of Arphaxad, which was the son of Sem, which was the son of Noe, which was the son of Lamech, ³⁷ which was the son of Mathusala, which was the son of Enoch, which was the son of Jared, which was the son of Maleleel, which was the son of Cainan, ³⁸ which was the son of Enos, which was the son of Seth, which was the son of Adam, which was the son of God.

4 And Jesus being full of the Holy Ghost returned from Jordan, and was led by the Spirit into the wilderness,

² being forty days tempted of the devil. And in those days he did eat nothing: and when they were ended, he afterward hungered. ³And the devil said unto him, 'If thou be the Son of God, command this stone that it be made bread.' ⁴And Jesus answered him, saying, 'It is written, "That man shall not live by bread alone, but by every word of God."'

⁵And the devil, taking him up into an high mountain, shewed unto him all the kingdoms of the world in a moment of time. ⁶And the devil said unto him, 'All this power will I give thee, and the glory of them; for that is delivered unto me, and to whomsoever I will I give it. ⁷If thou therefore wilt worship me, all shall be thine.' ⁸And Jesus answered and said unto him, 'Get thee behind me, Satan; for it is written, "Thou shalt worship the Lord thy God, and him only shalt thou serve."'

⁹And he brought him to Jerusalem, and set him on a pinnacle of the temple, and said unto him, 'If thou be the Son of God, cast thyself down from hence. ¹⁰For it is written, "He shall give his angels charge over thee, to keep thee: ¹¹and in their hands they shall bear thee up, lest at any time thou dash thy foot against a stone."' ¹²And Jesus answering said unto him, 'It is said, "Thou shalt not tempt the Lord thy God."' ¹³And when the devil had ended all the temptation, he departed from him for a season.

¹⁴And Jesus returned in the power of the Spirit into Galilee: and there went out a fame of him through all the region round about. ¹⁵And he taught in their synagogues, being glorified of all.

¹⁶And he came to Nazareth, where he had been brought up: and, as his custom was, he went into the synagogue on

the sabbath day, and stood up for to read. ¹⁷And there was delivered unto him the book of the prophet Esaias. And when he had opened the book, he found the place where it was written, ¹⁸'The Spirit of the Lord is upon me, because he hath anointed me to preach the gospel to the poor; he hath sent me to heal the brokenhearted, to preach deliverance to the captives, and recovering of sight to the blind, to set at liberty them that are bruised, ¹⁹to preach the acceptable year of the Lord.' ²⁰And he closed the book, and he gave it again to the minister, and sat down. And the eyes of all them that were in the synagogue were fastened on him. ²¹And he began to say unto them, 'This day is this scripture fulfilled in your ears.' ²²And all bare him witness, and wondered at the gracious words which proceeded out of his mouth. And they said, 'Is not this Joseph's son?' ²³And he said unto them, 'Ye will surely say unto me this proverb, "Physician, heal thyself: whatsoever we have heard done in Capernaum, do also here in thy country."' ²⁴And he said, 'Verily I say unto you, no prophet is accepted in his own country. ²⁵But I tell you of a truth, many widows were in Israel in the days of Elias, when the heaven was shut up three years and six months, when great famine was throughout all the land; ²⁶but unto none of them was Elias sent, save unto Sarepta, a city of Sidon, unto a woman that was a widow. ²⁷And many lepers were in Israel in the time of Eliseus the prophet; and none of them was cleansed, saving Naaman the Syrian.' ²⁸And all they in the synagogue, when they heard these things, were filled with wrath, ²⁹and rose up, and thrust him out of the city, and led him unto the brow of the hill whereon their city was built, that they might cast him down headlong. ³⁰But he passing through the midst of them went his way, ³¹and came down to Capernaum, a city of Galilee, and taught them on the sabbath days. ³²And they were astonished at his doctrine: for his word was with power.

³³And in the synagogue there was a man, which had a spirit of an unclean devil, and cried out with a loud voice, ³⁴saying, 'Let us alone; what have we to do with thee, thou Jesus of Nazareth? Art thou come to destroy us? I know thee who thou art; the Holy One of God.' ³⁵And Jesus rebuked him, saying, 'Hold thy peace, and come out of him.' And when the devil had thrown him in the midst, he came out of him, and hurt him not. ³⁶And they were all amazed, and spake among themselves, saying, 'What a word is this! For with authority and power he commandeth the unclean spirits, and they come out.' ³⁷And the fame of him went out into every place of the country round about.

³⁸And he arose out of the synagogue, and entered into Simon's house. And Simon's wife's mother was taken with a great fever; and they besought him for her. ³⁹And he stood over her, and rebuked the fever, and it left her; and immediately she arose and ministered unto them.

⁴⁰Now when the sun was setting, all they that had any sick with divers diseases brought them unto him; and he laid his hands on every one of them, and healed them. ⁴¹And devils also came out of many, crying out, and saying, 'Thou art Christ the Son of God.' And he rebuking them suffered them not to speak; for they knew that he was Christ. ⁴²And when it was day, he departed and went into a desert place; and the people sought him, and came unto him, and stayed him, that he should not depart from them. ⁴³And he said

unto them, 'I must preach the kingdom of God to other cities also: for therefore am I sent.' ⁴⁴And he preached in the synagogues of Galilee.

5 And it came to pass, that, as the people pressed upon him to hear the word of God, he stood by the lake of Gennesaret, ²and saw two ships standing by the lake; but the fishermen were gone out of them, and were washing their nets. ³And he entered into one of the ships, which was Simon's, and prayed him that he would thrust out a little from the land. And he sat down, and taught the people out of the ship. ⁴Now when he had left speaking, he said unto Simon, 'Launch out into the deep, and let down your nets for a draught.' ⁵And Simon answering said unto him, 'Master, we have toiled all the night, and have taken nothing; nevertheless at thy word I will let down the net.' ⁶And when they had this done, they inclosed a great multitude of fishes; and their net brake. ⁷And they beckoned unto their partners, which were in the other ship, that they should come and help them. And they came, and filled both the ships, so that they began to sink. ⁸When Simon Peter saw it, he fell down at Jesus' knees, saying, 'Depart from me; for I am a sinful man, O Lord.' ⁹For he was astonished, and all that were with him, at the draught of the fishes which they had taken. ¹⁰And so was also James, and John, the sons of Zebedee, which were partners with Simon. And Jesus said unto Simon, 'Fear not; from henceforth thou shalt catch men.' ¹¹And when they had brought their ships to land, they forsook all, and followed him.

¹²And it came to pass, when he was in a certain city, behold a man full of leprosy, who seeing Jesus fell on his face, and

besought him, saying, 'Lord, if thou wilt, thou canst make me clean.' ¹³And he put forth his hand, and touched him, saying, 'I will: be thou clean.' And immediately the leprosy departed from him. ¹⁴And he charged him to tell no man, 'But go, and shew thyself to the priest, and offer for thy cleansing, according as Moses commanded, for a testimony unto them.' ¹⁵But so much the more went there a fame abroad of him; and great multitudes came together to hear, and to be healed by him of their infirmities.

¹⁶And he withdrew himself into the wilderness, and prayed. ¹⁷And it came to pass on a certain day, as he was teaching, that there were Pharisees and doctors of the law sitting by, which were come out of every town of Galilee, and Judæa, and Jerusalem; and the power of the Lord was present to heal them.

¹⁸And, behold, men brought in a bed a man which was taken with a palsy: and they sought means to bring him in, and to lay him before him. ¹⁹And when they could not find by what way they might bring him in because of the multitude, they went upon the housetop, and let him down through the tiling with his couch into the midst before Jesus. ²⁰And when he saw their faith, he said unto him, 'Man, thy sins are forgiven thee.' ²¹And the scribes and the Pharisees began to reason, saying, 'Who is this which speaketh blasphemies? Who can forgive sins, but God alone?' ²²But when Jesus perceived their thoughts, he answering said unto them, 'What reason ye in your hearts? ²³Whether is easier, to say, "Thy sins be forgiven thee," or to say, "Rise up and walk"? ²⁴But that ye may know that the Son of man hath power upon earth to forgive sins (he said unto the sick of the palsy), I say

unto thee, "Arise, and take up thy couch, and go into thine house."' ²⁵And immediately he rose up before them, and took up that whereon he lay, and departed to his own house, glorifying God. ²⁶And they were all amazed, and they glorified God, and were filled with fear, saying, 'We have seen strange things today.'

²⁷And after these things he went forth, and saw a publican, named Levi, sitting at the receipt of custom; and he said unto him, 'Follow me.' ²⁸And he left all, rose up, and followed him. ²⁹And Levi made him a great feast in his own house; and there was a great company of publicans and of others that sat down with them. ³⁰But their scribes and Pharisees murmured against his disciples, saying, 'Why do ye eat and drink with publicans and sinners?' ³¹And Jesus answering said unto them, 'They that are whole need not a physician; but they that are sick. ³²I came not to call the righteous, but sinners to repentance.'

³³And they said unto him, 'Why do the disciples of John fast often, and make prayers, and likewise the disciples of the Pharisees; but thine eat and drink?' ³⁴And he said unto them, 'Can ye make the children of the bridechamber fast, while the bridegroom is with them? ³⁵But the days will come, when the bridegroom shall be taken away from them, and then shall they fast in those days.'

³⁶And he spake also a parable unto them: 'No man putteth a piece of a new garment upon an old; if otherwise, then both the new maketh a rent, and the piece that was taken out of the new agreeth not with the old. ³⁷And no man putteth new wine into old bottles; else the new wine will burst the bottles, and be spilled, and the bottles shall perish. ³⁸But new

wine must be put into new bottles; and both are preserved.
³⁹ No man also having drunk old wine straightway desireth
new: for he saith, "The old is better."'

6 And it came to pass on the second sabbath after the first,
that he went through the corn fields; and his disciples
plucked the ears of corn, and did eat, rubbing them in their
hands. ²And certain of the Pharisees said unto them, 'Why
do ye that which is not lawful to do on the sabbath days?'
³And Jesus answering them said, 'Have ye not read so much
as this, what David did, when himself was an hungred, and
they which were with him; ⁴how he went into the house of
God, and did take and eat the shewbread, and gave also to
them that were with him; which it is not lawful to eat but for
the priests alone?' ⁵And he said unto them that 'The Son of
man is Lord also of the sabbath.'

⁶And it came to pass also on another sabbath, that he
entered into the synagogue and taught; and there was a man
whose right hand was withered. ⁷And the scribes and Pharisees watched him, whether he would heal on the sabbath
day; that they might find an accusation against him. ⁸ But he
knew their thoughts, and said to the man which had the withered hand, 'Rise up, and stand forth in the midst.' And he
arose and stood forth. ⁹ Then said Jesus unto them, 'I will ask
you one thing: Is it lawful on the sabbath days to do good, or
to do evil? To save life, or to destroy it?' ¹⁰And looking
round about upon them all, he said unto the man, 'Stretch
forth thy hand.' And he did so; and his hand was restored
whole as the other. ¹¹And they were filled with madness; and
communed one with another what they might do to Jesus.

¹²And it came to pass in those days, that he went out into a mountain to pray, and continued all night in prayer to God. ¹³And when it was day, he called unto him his disciples: and of them he chose twelve, whom also he named apostles: ¹⁴Simon (whom he also named Peter) and Andrew his brother, James and John, Philip and Bartholomew, ¹⁵Matthew and Thomas, James the son of Alphæus, and Simon called Zelotes, ¹⁶and Judas the brother of James, and Judas Iscariot, which also was the traitor.

¹⁷And he came down with them, and stood in the plain, and the company of his disciples, and a great multitude of people out of all Judæa and Jerusalem, and from the sea coast of Tyre and Sidon, which came to hear him, and to be healed of their diseases; ¹⁸and they that were vexed with unclean spirits. And they were healed. ¹⁹And the whole multitude sought to touch him; for there went virtue out of him, and healed them all.

²⁰And he lifted up his eyes on his disciples, and said, 'Blessed be ye poor; for yours is the kingdom of God. ²¹Blessed are ye that hunger now; for ye shall be filled. Blessed are ye that weep now; for ye shall laugh. ²²Blessed are ye, when men shall hate you, and when they shall separate you from their company, and shall reproach you, and cast out your name as evil, for the Son of man's sake. ²³Rejoice ye in that day, and leap for joy; for, behold, your reward is great in heaven, for in the like manner did their fathers unto the prophets. ²⁴But woe unto you that are rich! For ye have received your consolation. ²⁵Woe unto you that are full! For ye shall hunger. Woe unto you that laugh now! For ye shall mourn and weep. ²⁶Woe unto you, when all men shall speak

well of you! For so did their fathers to the false prophets.

²⁷'But I say unto you which hear, Love your enemies, do good to them which hate you, ²⁸ bless them that curse you, and pray for them which despitefully use you. ²⁹And unto him that smiteth thee on the one cheek offer also the other; and him that taketh away thy cloke forbid not to take thy coat also. ³⁰ Give to every man that asketh of thee; and of him that taketh away thy goods ask them not again. ³¹And as ye would that men should do to you, do ye also to them likewise. ³² For if ye love them which love you, what thank have ye? For sinners also love those that love them. ³³And if ye do good to them which do good to you, what thank have ye? For sinners also do even the same. ³⁴And if ye lend to them of whom ye hope to receive, what thank have ye? For sinners also lend to sinners, to receive as much again. ³⁵ But love ye your enemies, and do good, and lend, hoping for nothing again; and your reward shall be great, and ye shall be the children of the Highest: for he is kind unto the unthankful and to the evil. ³⁶ Be ye therefore merciful, as your Father also is merciful. ³⁷ Judge not, and ye shall not be judged; condemn not, and ye shall not be condemned; forgive, and ye shall be forgiven; ³⁸ give, and it shall be given unto you; good measure, pressed down, and shaken together, and running over, shall men give into your bosom. For with the same measure that ye mete withal it shall be measured to you again.'

³⁹And he spake a parable unto them, 'Can the blind lead the blind? Shall they not both fall into the ditch? ⁴⁰ The disciple is not above his master: but every one that is perfect shall be as his master. ⁴¹And why beholdest thou the mote that is in thy brother's eye, but perceivest not the beam that is in

thine own eye? ⁴²Either how canst thou say to thy brother, "Brother, let me pull out the mote that is in thine eye," when thou thyself beholdest not the beam that is in thine own eye? Thou hypocrite, cast out first the beam out of thine own eye, and then shalt thou see clearly to pull out the mote that is in thy brother's eye. ⁴³For a good tree bringeth not forth corrupt fruit; neither doth a corrupt tree bring forth good fruit. ⁴⁴For every tree is known by his own fruit. For of thorns men do not gather figs, nor of a bramble bush gather they grapes. ⁴⁵A good man out of the good treasure of his heart bringeth forth that which is good; and an evil man out of the evil treasure of his heart bringeth forth that which is evil: for of the abundance of the heart his mouth speaketh.

⁴⁶'And why call ye me, "Lord, Lord," and do not the things which I say? ⁴⁷Whosoever cometh to me, and heareth my sayings, and doeth them, I will shew you to whom he is like. ⁴⁸He is like a man which built an house, and digged deep, and laid the foundation on a rock: and when the flood arose, the stream beat vehemently upon that house, and could not shake it: for it was founded upon a rock. ⁴⁹But he that heareth, and doeth not, is like a man that without a foundation built an house upon the earth; against which the stream did beat vehemently, and immediately it fell; and the ruin of that house was great.'

7 Now when he had ended all his sayings in the audience of the people, he entered into Capernaum. ²And a certain centurion's servant, who was dear unto him, was sick, and ready to die. ³And when he heard of Jesus, he sent unto him the elders of the Jews, beseeching him that he would

come and heal his servant. ⁴And when they came to Jesus, they besought him instantly, saying, that 'He was worthy for whom he should do this, ⁵for he loveth our nation, and he hath built us a synagogue.' ⁶Then Jesus went with them. And when he was now not far from the house, the centurion sent friends to him, saying unto him, 'Lord, trouble not thyself; for I am not worthy that thou shouldest enter under my roof. ⁷Wherefore neither thought I myself worthy to come unto thee; but say in a word, and my servant shall be healed. ⁸For I also am a man set under authority, having under me soldiers, and I say unto one, "Go," and he goeth; and to another, "Come," and he cometh; and to my servant, "Do this," and he doeth it.' ⁹When Jesus heard these things, he marvelled at him, and turned him about, and said unto the people that followed him, 'I say unto you, I have not found so great faith, no, not in Israel.' ¹⁰And they that were sent, returning to the house, found the servant whole that had been sick.

¹¹And it came to pass the day after, that he went into a city called Nain; and many of his disciples went with him, and much people. ¹²Now when he came nigh to the gate of the city, behold, there was a dead man carried out, the only son of his mother, and she was a widow; and much people of the city was with her. ¹³And when the Lord saw her, he had compassion on her, and said unto her, 'Weep not.' ¹⁴And he came and touched the bier: and they that bare him stood still. And he said, 'Young man, I say unto thee, Arise.' ¹⁵And he that was dead sat up, and began to speak. And he delivered him to his mother. ¹⁶And there came a fear on all: and they glorified God, saying, that 'a great prophet is risen up

among us'; and, that 'God hath visited his people.' ¹⁷And this rumour of him went forth throughout all Judæa, and throughout all the region round about. ¹⁸And the disciples of John shewed him of all these things.

¹⁹And John calling unto him two of his disciples sent them to Jesus, saying, 'Art thou he that should come? Or look we for another?' ²⁰When the men were come unto him, they said, 'John Baptist hath sent us unto thee, saying, "Art thou he that should come? Or look we for another?"' ²¹And in that same hour he cured many of their infirmities and plagues, and of evil spirits; and unto many that were blind he gave sight. ²²Then Jesus answering said unto them, 'Go your way, and tell John what things ye have seen and heard; how that the blind see, the lame walk, the lepers are cleansed, the deaf hear, the dead are raised, to the poor the gospel is preached. ²³And blessed is he, whosoever shall not be offended in me.'

²⁴And when the messengers of John were departed, he began to speak unto the people concerning John, 'What went ye out into the wilderness for to see? A reed shaken with the wind? ²⁵But what went ye out for to see? A man clothed in soft raiment? Behold, they which are gorgeously apparelled, and live delicately, are in kings' courts. ²⁶But what went ye out for to see? A prophet? Yea, I say unto you, and much more than a prophet. ²⁷This is he, of whom it is written, "Behold, I send my messenger before thy face, which shall prepare thy way before thee." ²⁸For I say unto you, Among those that are born of women there is not a greater prophet than John the Baptist: but he that is least in the kingdom of God is greater than he.' ²⁹And all the people that heard him, and the publicans, justified God, being baptized with the baptism of John.

³⁰ But the Pharisees and lawyers rejected the counsel of God against themselves, being not baptized of him.

³¹And the Lord said, 'Whereunto then shall I liken the men of this generation? And to what are they like? ³²They are like unto children sitting in the marketplace, and calling one to another, and saying, "We have piped unto you, and ye have not danced; we have mourned to you, and ye have not wept." ³³For John the Baptist came neither eating bread nor drinking wine; and ye say, "He hath a devil." ³⁴The Son of man is come eating and drinking; and ye say, "Behold a gluttonous man, and a winebibber, a friend of publicans and sinners!" ³⁵But wisdom is justified of all her children.'

³⁶And one of the Pharisees desired him that he would eat with him. And he went into the Pharisee's house, and sat down to meat. ³⁷And, behold, a woman in the city, which was a sinner, when she knew that Jesus sat at meat in the Pharisee's house, brought an alabaster box of ointment, ³⁸and stood at his feet behind him weeping, and began to wash his feet with tears, and did wipe them with the hairs of her head, and kissed his feet, and anointed them with the ointment. ³⁹Now when the Pharisee which had bidden him saw it, he spake within himself, saying, 'This man, if he were a prophet, would have known who and what manner of woman this is that toucheth him: for she is a sinner.' ⁴⁰And Jesus answering said unto him, 'Simon, I have somewhat to say unto thee.' And he saith, 'Master, say on.' ⁴¹'There was a certain creditor which had two debtors: the one owed five hundred pence, and the other fifty. ⁴²And when they had nothing to pay, he frankly forgave them both. Tell me therefore, which of them will love him most?' ⁴³Simon answered

and said, 'I suppose that he, to whom he forgave most.' And he said unto him, 'Thou hast rightly judged.' ⁴⁴And he turned to the woman, and said unto Simon, 'Seest thou this woman? I entered into thine house, thou gavest me no water for my feet: but she hath washed my feet with tears, and wiped them with the hairs of her head. ⁴⁵ Thou gavest me no kiss: but this woman since the time I came in hath not ceased to kiss my feet. ⁴⁶ My head with oil thou didst not anoint: but this woman hath anointed my feet with ointment. ⁴⁷ Wherefore I say unto thee, her sins, which are many, are forgiven; for she loved much; but to whom little is forgiven, the same loveth little.' ⁴⁸And he said unto her, 'Thy sins are forgiven.' ⁴⁹And they that sat at meat with him began to say within themselves, 'Who is this that forgiveth sins also?' ⁵⁰And he said to the woman, 'Thy faith hath saved thee; go in peace.'

8 And it came to pass afterward, that he went throughout every city and village, preaching and shewing the glad tidings of the kingdom of God; and the twelve were with him, ²and certain women, which had been healed of evil spirits and infirmities: Mary called Magdalene, out of whom went seven devils, ³and Joanna the wife of Chuza Herod's steward, and Susanna, and many others, which ministered unto him of their substance.

⁴And when much people were gathered together, and were come to him out of every city, he spake by a parable: ⁵'A sower went out to sow his seed; and as he sowed, some fell by the way side; and it was trodden down, and the fowls of the air devoured it. ⁶And some fell upon a rock; and as soon as it was sprung up, it withered away, because it lacked

moisture. [7]And some fell among thorns; and the thorns sprang up with it, and choked it. [8]And other fell on good ground, and sprang up, and bare fruit an hundred-fold.' And when he had said these things, he cried, 'He that hath ears to hear, let him hear.'

[9]And his disciples asked him, saying, 'What might this parable be?' [10]And he said, 'Unto you it is given to know the mysteries of the kingdom of God; but to others in parables, that seeing they might not see, and hearing they might not understand. [11]Now the parable is this: The seed is the word of God. [12]Those by the way side are they that hear; then cometh the devil, and taketh away the word out of their hearts, lest they should believe and be saved. [13]They on the rock are they, which, when they hear, receive the word with joy; and these have no root, which for a while believe, and in time of temptation fall away. [14]And that which fell among thorns are they, which, when they have heard, go forth, and are choked with cares and riches and pleasures of this life, and bring no fruit to perfection. [15]But that on the good ground are they, which in an honest and good heart, having heard the word, keep it, and bring forth fruit with patience.

[16]'No man, when he hath lighted a candle, covereth it with a vessel, or putteth it under a bed; but setteth it on a candle-stick, that they which enter in may see the light. [17]For nothing is secret, that shall not be made manifest; neither any thing hid, that shall not be known and come abroad. [18]Take heed therefore how ye hear; for whosoever hath, to him shall be given; and whosoever hath not, from him shall be taken even that which he seemeth to have.'

[19]Then came to him his mother and his brethren, and

could not come at him for the press. ²⁰And it was told him by certain which said, 'Thy mother and thy brethren stand without, desiring to see thee.' ²¹And he answered and said unto them, 'My mother and my brethren are these which hear the word of God, and do it.'

²² Now it came to pass on a certain day, that he went into a ship with his disciples; and he said unto them, 'Let us go over unto the other side of the lake.' And they launched forth. ²³But as they sailed he fell asleep; and there came down a storm of wind on the lake; and they were filled with water, and were in jeopardy. ²⁴And they came to him, and awoke him, saying, 'Master, master, we perish.' Then he arose, and rebuked the wind and the raging of the water; and they ceased, and there was a calm. ²⁵And he said unto them, 'Where is your faith?' And they being afraid wondered, saying one to another, 'What manner of man is this! For he commandeth even the winds and water, and they obey him.'

²⁶And they arrived at the country of the Gadarenes, which is over against Galilee. ²⁷And when he went forth to land, there met him out of the city a certain man, which had devils long time, and ware no clothes, neither abode in any house, but in the tombs. ²⁸ When he saw Jesus, he cried out, and fell down before him, and with a loud voice said, 'What have I to do with thee, Jesus, thou Son of God most high? I beseech thee, torment me not.' ²⁹(For he had commanded the unclean spirit to come out of the man. For often-times it had caught him; and he was kept bound with chains and in fetters; and he brake the bands, and was driven of the devil into the wilderness.) ³⁰And Jesus asked him, saying, 'What is thy name?' And he said, 'Legion', because many devils were

entered into him. ³¹And they besought him that he would not command them to go out into the deep.

³²And there was there an herd of many swine feeding on the mountain; and they besought him that he would suffer them to enter into them. And he suffered them. ³³Then went the devils out of the man, and entered into the swine; and the herd ran violently down a steep place into the lake, and were choked. ³⁴When they that fed them saw what was done, they fled, and went and told it in the city and in the country. ³⁵Then they went out to see what was done; and came to Jesus, and found the man, out of whom the devils were departed, sitting at the feet of Jesus, clothed, and in his right mind; and they were afraid. ³⁶They also which saw it told them by what means he that was possessed of the devils was healed.

³⁷Then the whole multitude of the country of the Gadarenes round about besought him to depart from them; for they were taken with great fear: and he went up into the ship, and returned back again. ³⁸Now the man out of whom the devils were departed besought him that he might be with him; but Jesus sent him away, saying, ³⁹'Return to thine own house, and shew how great things God hath done unto thee.' And he went his way, and published throughout the whole city how great things Jesus had done unto him. ⁴⁰And it came to pass, that, when Jesus was returned, the people gladly received him; for they were all waiting for him.

⁴¹And, behold, there came a man named Jairus, and he was a ruler of the synagogue; and he fell down at Jesus' feet, and besought him that he would come into his house. ⁴²For he had one only daughter, about twelve years of age, and

she lay a dying. But as he went the people thronged him.

⁴³And a woman having an issue of blood twelve years, which had spent all her living upon physicians, neither could be healed of any, ⁴⁴came behind him, and touched the border of his garment: and immediately her issue of blood stanched. ⁴⁵And Jesus said, 'Who touched me?' When all denied, Peter and they that were with him said, 'Master, the multitude throng thee and press thee, and sayest thou, "Who touched me?"' ⁴⁶And Jesus said, 'Somebody hath touched me; for I perceive that virtue is gone out of me.' ⁴⁷And when the woman saw that she was not hid, she came trembling, and falling down before him, she declared unto him before all the people for what cause she had touched him, and how she was healed immediately. ⁴⁸And he said unto her, 'Daughter, be of good comfort: thy faith hath made thee whole; go in peace.'

⁴⁹While he yet spake, there cometh one from the ruler of the synagogue's house, saying to him, 'Thy daughter is dead; trouble not the Master.' ⁵⁰But when Jesus heard it, he answered him, saying, 'Fear not: believe only, and she shall be made whole.' ⁵¹And when he came into the house, he suffered no man to go in, save Peter, and James, and John, and the father and the mother of the maiden. ⁵²And all wept, and bewailed her; but he said, 'Weep not; she is not dead, but sleepeth.' ⁵³And they laughed him to scorn, knowing that she was dead. ⁵⁴And he put them all out, and took her by the hand, and called, saying, 'Maid, arise.' ⁵⁵And her spirit came again, and she arose straightway: and he commanded to give her meat. ⁵⁶And her parents were astonished: but he charged them that they should tell no man what was done.

9 Then he called his twelve disciples together, and gave them power and authority over all devils, and to cure diseases. ²And he sent them to preach the kingdom of God, and to heal the sick. ³And he said unto them, 'Take nothing for your journey, neither staves, nor scrip, neither bread, neither money; neither have two coats apiece. ⁴And whatsoever house ye enter into, there abide, and thence depart. ⁵And whosoever will not receive you, when ye go out of that city, shake off the very dust from your feet for a testimony against them.' ⁶And they departed, and went through the towns, preaching the gospel, and healing every where.

⁷ Now Herod the tetrarch heard of all that was done by him: and he was perplexed, because that it was said of some, that John was risen from the dead; ⁸and of some, that Elias had appeared; and of others, that one of the old prophets was risen again. ⁹And Herod said, 'John have I beheaded: but who is this, of whom I hear such things?' And he desired to see him.

¹⁰And the apostles, when they were returned, told him all that they had done. And he took them, and went aside privately into a desert place belonging to the city called Bethsaida. ¹¹And the people, when they knew it, followed him: and he received them, and spake unto them of the kingdom of God, and healed them that had need of healing. ¹²And when the day began to wear away, then came the twelve, and said unto him, 'Send the multitude away, that they may go into the towns and country round about, and lodge, and get victuals: for we are here in a desert place.' ¹³ But he said unto them, 'Give ye them to eat.' And they said, 'We have no more but five loaves and two fishes; except we should go

and buy meat for all this people.' ¹⁴ For they were about five thousand men. And he said to his disciples, 'Make them sit down by fifties in a company.' ¹⁵ And they did so, and made them all sit down. ¹⁶ Then he took the five loaves and the two fishes, and looking up to heaven, he blessed them, and brake, and gave to the disciples to set before the multitude. ¹⁷ And they did eat, and were all filled: and there was taken up of fragments that remained to them twelve baskets.

¹⁸ And it came to pass, as he was alone praying, his disciples were with him: and he asked them, saying, 'Whom say the people that I am?' ¹⁹ They answering said, 'John the Baptist; but some say, Elias; and others say, that one of the old prophets is risen again.' ²⁰ He said unto them, 'But whom say ye that I am?' Peter answering said, 'The Christ of God.' ²¹ And he straitly charged them, and commanded them to tell no man that thing, ²² saying, 'The Son of man must suffer many things, and be rejected of the elders and chief priests and scribes, and be slain, and be raised the third day.'

²³ And he said to them all, 'If any man will come after me, let him deny himself, and take up his cross daily, and follow me. ²⁴ For whosoever will save his life shall lose it; but whosoever will lose his life for my sake, the same shall save it. ²⁵ For what is a man advantaged, if he gain the whole world, and lose himself, or be cast away? ²⁶ For whosoever shall be ashamed of me and of my words, of him shall the Son of man be ashamed, when he shall come in his own glory, and in his Father's, and of the holy angels. ²⁷ But I tell you of a truth, there be some standing here, which shall not taste of death, till they see the kingdom of God.'

²⁸ And it came to pass about an eight days after these

sayings, he took Peter and John and James, and went up into a mountain to pray. ²⁹And as he prayed, the fashion of his countenance was altered, and his raiment was white and glistering. ³⁰And, behold, there talked with him two men, which were Moses and Elias, ³¹who appeared in glory, and spake of his decease which he should accomplish at Jerusalem. ³²But Peter and they that were with him were heavy with sleep; and when they were awake, they saw his glory, and the two men that stood with him. ³³And it came to pass, as they departed from him, Peter said unto Jesus, 'Master, it is good for us to be here: and let us make three tabernacles: one for thee, and one for Moses, and one for Elias,' not knowing what he said. ³⁴While he thus spake, there came a cloud, and overshadowed them; and they feared as they entered into the cloud. ³⁵And there came a voice out of the cloud, saying, 'This is my beloved Son: hear him.' ³⁶And when the voice was past, Jesus was found alone. And they kept it close, and told no man in those days any of those things which they had seen.

³⁷And it came to pass that on the next day, when they were come down from the hill, much people met him. ³⁸And, behold, a man of the company cried out, saying, 'Master, I beseech thee, look upon my son; for he is mine only child. ³⁹And, lo, a spirit taketh him, and he suddenly crieth out; and it teareth him that he foameth again, and bruising him hardly departeth from him. ⁴⁰And I besought thy disciples to cast him out; and they could not.' ⁴¹And Jesus answering said, 'O faithless and perverse generation, how long shall I be with you, and suffer you? Bring thy son hither.' ⁴²And as he was yet a coming, the devil threw him down, and tare him. And

Jesus rebuked the unclean spirit, and healed the child, and delivered him again to his father.

⁴³And they were all amazed at the mighty power of God. But while they wondered every one at all things which Jesus did, he said unto his disciples, ⁴⁴'Let these sayings sink down into your ears: for the Son of man shall be delivered into the hands of men.' ⁴⁵But they understood not this saying, and it was hid from them, that they perceived it not: and they feared to ask him of that saying.

⁴⁶Then there arose a reasoning among them, which of them should be greatest. ⁴⁷And Jesus, perceiving the thought of their heart, took a child, and set him by him, ⁴⁸and said unto them, 'Whosoever shall receive this child in my name receiveth me: and whosoever shall receive me receiveth him that sent me; for he that is least among you all, the same shall be great.'

⁴⁹And John answered and said, 'Master, we saw one casting out devils in thy name; and we forbad him, because he followeth not with us.' ⁵⁰And Jesus said unto him, 'Forbid him not: for he that is not against us is for us.'

⁵¹And it came to pass, when the time was come that he should be received up, he stedfastly set his face to go to Jerusalem, ⁵²and sent messengers before his face: and they went, and entered into a village of the Samaritans, to make ready for him. ⁵³And they did not receive him, because his face was as though he would go to Jerusalem. ⁵⁴And when his disciples James and John saw this, they said, 'Lord, wilt thou that we command fire to come down from heaven, and consume them, even as Elias did?' ⁵⁵But he turned, and rebuked them, and said, 'Ye know not what manner of spirit ye are of. ⁵⁶For

the Son of man is not come to destroy men's lives, but to save them.' And they went to another village.

⁵⁷And it came to pass, that, as they went in the way, a certain man said unto him, 'Lord, I will follow thee whithersoever thou goest.' ⁵⁸And Jesus said unto him, 'Foxes have holes, and birds of the air have nests; but the Son of man hath not where to lay his head.' ⁵⁹And he said unto another, 'Follow me.' But he said, 'Lord, suffer me first to go and bury my father.' ⁶⁰Jesus said unto him, 'Let the dead bury their dead; but go thou and preach the kingdom of God.' ⁶¹And another also said, 'Lord, I will follow thee; but let me first go bid them farewell, which are at home at my house.' ⁶²And Jesus said unto him, 'No man, having put his hand to the plough, and looking back, is fit for the kingdom of God.'

10 After these things the Lord appointed other seventy also, and sent them two and two before his face into every city and place, whither he himself would come. ²Therefore said he unto them, 'The harvest truly is great, but the labourers are few; pray ye therefore the Lord of the harvest, that he would send forth labourers into his harvest. ³Go your ways: behold, I send you forth as lambs among wolves. ⁴Carry neither purse, nor scrip, nor shoes: and salute no man by the way. ⁵And into whatsoever house ye enter, first say, "Peace be to this house." ⁶And if the son of peace be there, your peace shall rest upon it: if not, it shall turn to you again. ⁷And in the same house remain, eating and drinking such things as they give: for the labourer is worthy of his hire. Go not from house to house. ⁸And into whatsoever city ye enter, and they receive you, eat such things as are set

before you. ⁹And heal the sick that are therein, and say unto them, "The kingdom of God is come nigh unto you." ¹⁰But into whatsoever city ye enter, and they receive you not, go your ways out into the streets of the same, and say, ¹¹"Even the very dust of your city, which cleaveth on us, we do wipe off against you; notwithstanding be ye sure of this, that the kingdom of God is come nigh unto you." ¹²But I say unto you, that it shall be more tolerable in that day for Sodom, than for that city. ¹³Woe unto thee, Chorazin! Woe unto thee, Bethsaida! For if the mighty works had been done in Tyre and Sidon, which have been done in you, they had a great while ago repented, sitting in sackcloth and ashes. ¹⁴But it shall be more tolerable for Tyre and Sidon at the judgment, than for you. ¹⁵And thou, Capernaum, which art exalted to heaven, shalt be thrust down to hell. ¹⁶He that heareth you heareth me; and he that despiseth you despiseth me; and he that despiseth me despiseth him that sent me.'

¹⁷And the seventy returned again with joy, saying, 'Lord, even the devils are subject unto us through thy name.' ¹⁸And he said unto them, 'I beheld Satan as lightning fall from heaven. ¹⁹Behold, I give unto you power to tread on serpents and scorpions, and over all the power of the enemy; and nothing shall by any means hurt you. ²⁰Notwithstanding in this rejoice not, that the spirits are subject unto you; but rather rejoice, because your names are written in heaven.'

²¹In that hour Jesus rejoiced in spirit, and said, 'I thank thee, O Father, Lord of heaven and earth, that thou hast hid these things from the wise and prudent, and hast revealed them unto babes: even so, Father; for so it seemed good in thy sight. ²²All things are delivered to me of my Father; and

no man knoweth who the Son is, but the Father; and who the Father is, but the Son, and he to whom the Son will reveal him.'

²³And he turned him unto his disciples, and said privately, 'Blessed are the eyes which see the things that ye see. ²⁴For I tell you that many prophets and kings have desired to see those things which ye see, and have not seen them; and to hear those things which ye hear, and have not heard them.'

²⁵And, behold, a certain lawyer stood up, and tempted him, saying, 'Master, what shall I do to inherit eternal life?' ²⁶He said unto him, 'What is written in the law? How readest thou?' ²⁷And he answering said, 'Thou shalt love the Lord thy God with all thy heart, and with all thy soul, and with all thy strength, and with all thy mind; and thy neighbour as thyself.' ²⁸And he said unto him, 'Thou hast answered right: this do, and thou shalt live.' ²⁹But he, willing to justify himself, said unto Jesus, 'And who is my neighbour?' ³⁰And Jesus answering said, 'A certain man went down from Jerusalem to Jericho, and fell among thieves, which stripped him of his raiment, and wounded him, and departed, leaving him half dead. ³¹And by chance there came down a certain priest that way: and when he saw him, he passed by on the other side. ³²And likewise a Levite, when he was at the place, came and looked on him, and passed by on the other side. ³³But a certain Samaritan, as he journeyed, came where he was; and when he saw him, he had compassion on him, ³⁴and went to him, and bound up his wounds, pouring in oil and wine, and set him on his own beast, and brought him to an inn, and took care of him. ³⁵And on the morrow when he departed, he took out two pence, and gave them to the host, and said

unto him, "Take care of him; and whatsoever thou spendest more, when I come again, I will repay thee." ³⁶ Which now of these three, thinkest thou, was neighbour unto him that fell among the thieves?' ³⁷And he said, 'He that shewed mercy on him.' Then said Jesus unto him, 'Go, and do thou likewise.'

³⁸ Now it came to pass, as they went, that he entered into a certain village: and a certain woman named Martha received him into her house. ³⁹And she had a sister called Mary, which also sat at Jesus' feet, and heard his word. ⁴⁰But Martha was cumbered about much serving, and came to him, and said, 'Lord, dost thou not care that my sister hath left me to serve alone? Bid her therefore that she help me.' ⁴¹And Jesus answered and said unto her, 'Martha, Martha, thou art careful and troubled about many things, ⁴² but one thing is needful; and Mary hath chosen that good part, which shall not be taken away from her.'

11 And it came to pass, that, as he was praying in a certain place, when he ceased, one of his disciples said unto him, 'Lord, teach us to pray, as John also taught his disciples.' ²And he said unto them, 'When ye pray, say,

> Our Father which art in heaven,
>> Hallowed be thy name.
>>> Thy kingdom come.
>>> Thy will be done, as in heaven, so in earth.
> ³ Give us day by day our daily bread.
> ⁴And forgive us our sins;
>> for we also forgive every one
>>> that is indebted to us.

And lead us not into temptation;
but deliver us from evil.'

⁵And he said unto them, 'Which of you shall have a friend,
and shall go unto him at midnight, and say unto him, "Friend,
lend me three loaves; ⁶for a friend of mine in his journey is
come to me, and I have nothing to set before him?" ⁷And he
from within shall answer and say, "Trouble me not: the door
is now shut, and my children are with me in bed; I cannot
rise and give thee." ⁸I say unto you, though he will not rise
and give him, because he is his friend, yet because of his im-
portunity he will rise and give him as many as he needeth.

⁹'And I say unto you, ask, and it shall be given you; seek,
and ye shall find; knock, and it shall be opened unto you.
¹⁰For every one that asketh receiveth; and he that seeketh
findeth; and to him that knocketh it shall be opened. ¹¹If a
son shall ask bread of any of you that is a father, will he give
him a stone? Or if he ask a fish, will he for a fish give him a
serpent? ¹²Or if he shall ask an egg, will he offer him a scor-
pion? ¹³If ye then, being evil, know how to give good gifts
unto your children, how much more shall your heavenly
Father give the Holy Spirit to them that ask him?'

¹⁴And he was casting out a devil, and it was dumb. And it
came to pass, when the devil was gone out, the dumb spake;
and the people wondered. ¹⁵But some of them said, 'He cast-
eth out devils through Beelzebub the chief of the devils.'
¹⁶And others, tempting him, sought of him a sign from heaven.
¹⁷But he, knowing their thoughts, said unto them, 'Every
kingdom divided against itself is brought to desolation; and
a house divided against a house falleth. ¹⁸If Satan also be

divided against himself, how shall his kingdom stand? Because ye say that I cast out devils through Beelzebub. ¹⁹And if I by Beelzebub cast out devils, by whom do your sons cast them out? Therefore shall they be your judges. ²⁰But if I with the finger of God cast out devils, no doubt the kingdom of God is come upon you. ²¹When a strong man armed keepeth his palace, his goods are in peace. ²²But when a stronger man than he shall come upon him, and overcome him, he taketh from him all his armour wherein he trusted, and divideth his spoils. ²³He that is not with me is against me; and he that gathereth not with me scattereth. ²⁴When the unclean spirit is gone out of a man, he walketh through dry places, seeking rest; and finding none, he saith, "I will return unto my house whence I came out." ²⁵And when he cometh, he findeth it swept and garnished. ²⁶Then goeth he, and taketh to him seven other spirits more wicked than himself; and they enter in, and dwell there; and the last state of that man is worse than the first.'

²⁷And it came to pass, as he spake these things, a certain woman of the company lifted up her voice, and said unto him, 'Blessed is the womb that bare thee, and the paps which thou hast sucked.' ²⁸But he said, 'Yea rather, blessed are they that hear the word of God, and keep it.'

²⁹And when the people were gathered thick together, he began to say, 'This is an evil generation: they seek a sign; and there shall no sign be given it, but the sign of Jonas the prophet. ³⁰For as Jonas was a sign unto the Ninevites, so shall also the Son of man be to this generation. ³¹The queen of the south shall rise up in the judgment with the men of this generation, and condemn them; for she came from the

utmost parts of the earth to hear the wisdom of Solomon; and, behold, a greater than Solomon is here. ³² The men of Nineve shall rise up in the judgment with this generation, and shall condemn it; for they repented at the preaching of Jonas; and, behold, a greater than Jonas is here. ³³ No man, when he hath lighted a candle, putteth it in a secret place, neither under a bushel, but on a candlestick, that they which come in may see the light. ³⁴ The light of the body is the eye: therefore when thine eye is single, thy whole body also is full of light, but when thine eye is evil, thy body also is full of darkness. ³⁵ Take heed therefore that the light which is in thee be not darkness. ³⁶ If thy whole body therefore be full of light, having no part dark, the whole shall be full of light, as when the bright shining of a candle doth give thee light.'

³⁷ And as he spake, a certain Pharisee besought him to dine with him; and he went in, and sat down to meat. ³⁸ And when the Pharisee saw it, he marvelled that he had not first washed before dinner. ³⁹ And the Lord said unto him, 'Now do ye Pharisees make clean the outside of the cup and the platter; but your inward part is full of ravening and wickedness. ⁴⁰ Ye fools, did not he that made that which is without make that which is within also? ⁴¹ But rather give alms of such things as ye have; and, behold, all things are clean unto you. ⁴² But woe unto you, Pharisees! For ye tithe mint and rue and all manner of herbs, and pass over judgment and the love of God; these ought ye to have done, and not to leave the other undone. ⁴³ Woe unto you, Pharisees! For ye love the uppermost seats in the synagogues, and greetings in the markets. ⁴⁴ Woe unto you, scribes and Pharisees, hypocrites! For ye are as graves which appear not, and the men

that walk over them are not aware of them.'

⁴⁵ Then answered one of the lawyers, and said unto him, 'Master, thus saying thou reproachest us also.' ⁴⁶And he said, 'Woe unto you also, ye lawyers! For ye lade men with burdens grievous to be borne, and ye yourselves touch not the burdens with one of your fingers. ⁴⁷Woe unto you! For ye build the sepulchres of the prophets, and your fathers killed them. ⁴⁸Truly ye bear witness that ye allow the deeds of your fathers; for they indeed killed them, and ye build their sepulchres. ⁴⁹Therefore also said the wisdom of God, "I will send them prophets and apostles, and some of them they shall slay and persecute," ⁵⁰that the blood of all the prophets, which was shed from the foundation of the world, may be required of this generation; ⁵¹from the blood of Abel unto the blood of Zacharias, which perished between the altar and the temple: verily I say unto you, it shall be required of this generation. ⁵²Woe unto you, lawyers! For ye have taken away the key of knowledge; ye entered not in yourselves, and them that were entering in ye hindered.'

⁵³And as he said these things unto them, the scribes and the Pharisees began to urge him vehemently, and to provoke him to speak of many things: ⁵⁴laying wait for him, and seeking to catch something out of his mouth, that they might accuse him.

12 In the mean time, when there were gathered together an innumerable multitude of people, insomuch that they trode one upon another, he began to say unto his disciples first of all, 'Beware ye of the leaven of the Pharisees, which is hypocrisy. ²For there is nothing covered, that shall not be revealed; neither hid, that shall not be known. ³Therefore

whatsoever ye have spoken in darkness shall be heard in the light; and that which ye have spoken in the ear in closets shall be proclaimed upon the housetops. ⁴And I say unto you my friends, be not afraid of them that kill the body, and after that have no more that they can do. ⁵But I will forewarn you whom ye shall fear: fear him, which after he hath killed hath power to cast into hell; yea, I say unto you, Fear him. ⁶Are not five sparrows sold for two farthings, and not one of them is forgotten before God? ⁷But even the very hairs of your head are all numbered. Fear not therefore: ye are of more value than many sparrows. ⁸Also I say unto you, whosoever shall confess me before men, him shall the Son of man also confess before the angels of God; ⁹ but he that denieth me before men shall be denied before the angels of God. ¹⁰And whosoever shall speak a word against the Son of man, it shall be forgiven him; but unto him that blasphemeth against the Holy Ghost it shall not be forgiven. ¹¹And when they bring you unto the synagogues, and unto magistrates, and powers, take ye no thought how or what thing ye shall answer, or what ye shall say. ¹²For the Holy Ghost shall teach you in the same hour what ye ought to say.'

¹³And one of the company said unto him, 'Master, speak to my brother, that he divide the inheritance with me.' ¹⁴And he said unto him, 'Man, who made me a judge or a divider over you?' ¹⁵And he said unto them, 'Take heed, and beware of covetousness; for a man's life consisteth not in the abundance of the things which he possesseth.' ¹⁶And he spake a parable unto them, saying, 'The ground of a certain rich man brought forth plentifully, ¹⁷and he thought within himself, saying, "What shall I do, because I have no room where to bestow

my fruits?" ¹⁸And he said, "This will I do: I will pull down my barns, and build greater; and there will I bestow all my fruits and my goods. ¹⁹And I will say to my soul, Soul, thou hast much goods laid up for many years; take thine ease, eat, drink, and be merry." ²⁰But God said unto him, "Thou fool, this night thy soul shall be required of thee; then whose shall those things be, which thou hast provided?" ²¹So is he that layeth up treasure for himself, and is not rich toward God.'

²²And he said unto his disciples, 'Therefore I say unto you, take no thought for your life, what ye shall eat; neither for the body, what ye shall put on. ²³The life is more than meat, and the body is more than raiment. ²⁴Consider the ravens, for they neither sow nor reap; which neither have storehouse nor barn; and God feedeth them: how much more are ye better than the fowls? ²⁵And which of you with taking thought can add to his stature one cubit? ²⁶If ye then be not able to do that thing which is least, why take ye thought for the rest? ²⁷Consider the lilies how they grow: they toil not, they spin not; and yet I say unto you, that Solomon in all his glory was not arrayed like one of these. ²⁸If then God so clothe the grass, which is today in the field, and tomorrow is cast into the oven, how much more will he clothe you, O ye of little faith? ²⁹And seek not ye what ye shall eat, or what ye shall drink, neither be ye of doubtful mind. ³⁰For all these things do the nations of the world seek after: and your Father knoweth that ye have need of these things.

³¹'But rather seek ye the kingdom of God; and all these things shall be added unto you. ³²Fear not, little flock; for it is your Father's good pleasure to give you the kingdom. ³³Sell that ye have, and give alms; provide yourselves bags

which wax not old, a treasure in the heavens that faileth not, where no thief approacheth, neither moth corrupteth. ³⁴ For where your treasure is, there will your heart be also. ³⁵ Let your loins be girded about, and your lights burning; ³⁶ and ye yourselves like unto men that wait for their lord, when he will return from the wedding; that when he cometh and knocketh, they may open unto him immediately. ³⁷ Blessed are those servants whom the lord when he cometh shall find watching: verily I say unto you that he shall gird himself, and make them to sit down to meat, and will come forth and serve them. ³⁸ And if he shall come in the second watch, or come in the third watch, and find them so, blessed are those servants. ³⁹ And this know, that if the goodman of the house had known what hour the thief would come, he would have watched, and not have suffered his house to be broken through. ⁴⁰ Be ye therefore ready also: for the Son of man cometh at an hour when ye think not.'

⁴¹ Then Peter said unto him, 'Lord, speakest thou this parable unto us, or even to all?' ⁴² And the Lord said, 'Who then is that faithful and wise steward, whom his lord shall make ruler over his household, to give them their portion of meat in due season? ⁴³ Blessed is that servant, whom his lord when he cometh shall find so doing. ⁴⁴ Of a truth I say unto you that he will make him ruler over all that he hath. ⁴⁵ But and if that servant say in his heart, "My lord delayeth his coming," and shall begin to beat the menservants and maidens, and to eat and drink, and to be drunken, ⁴⁶ the lord of that servant will come in a day when he looketh not for him, and at an hour when he is not aware, and will cut him in sunder, and will appoint him his portion with the unbelievers. ⁴⁷ And that servant, which

knew his lord's will, and prepared not himself, neither did according to his will, shall be beaten with many stripes. ⁴⁸ But he that knew not, and did commit things worthy of stripes, shall be beaten with few stripes. For unto whomsoever much is given, of him shall be much required: and to whom men have committed much, of him they will ask the more.

⁴⁹ 'I am come to send fire on the earth; and what will I, if it be already kindled? ⁵⁰ But I have a baptism to be baptized with; and how am I straitened till it be accomplished! ⁵¹ Suppose ye that I am come to give peace on earth? I tell you, nay; but rather division. ⁵² For from henceforth there shall be five in one house divided, three against two, and two against three. ⁵³ The father shall be divided against the son, and the son against the father; the mother against the daughter, and the daughter against the mother; the mother in law against her daughter in law, and the daughter in law against her mother in law.'

⁵⁴ And he said also to the people, 'When ye see a cloud rise out of the west, straightway ye say, "There cometh a shower," and so it is. ⁵⁵ And when ye see the south wind blow, ye say, "There will be heat," and it cometh to pass. ⁵⁶ Ye hypocrites, ye can discern the face of the sky and of the earth; but how is it that ye do not discern this time? ⁵⁷ Yea, and why even of yourselves judge ye not what is right?

⁵⁸ 'When thou goest with thine adversary to the magistrate, as thou art in the way, give diligence that thou mayest be delivered from him; lest he hale thee to the judge, and the judge deliver thee to the officer, and the officer cast thee into prison. ⁵⁹ I tell thee, thou shalt not depart thence, till thou hast paid the very last mite.'

13 There were present at that season some that told him of the Galilæans, whose blood Pilate had mingled with their sacrifices. ²And Jesus answering said unto them, 'Suppose ye that these Galilæans were sinners above all the Galilæans, because they suffered such things? ³I tell you, nay: but, except ye repent, ye shall all likewise perish. ⁴Or those eighteen, upon whom the tower in Siloam fell, and slew them, think ye that they were sinners above all men that dwelt in Jerusalem? ⁵I tell you, nay: but, except ye repent, ye shall all likewise perish.'

⁶He spake also this parable: 'A certain man had a fig tree planted in his vineyard; and he came and sought fruit thereon, and found none. ⁷Then said he unto the dresser of his vineyard, "Behold, these three years I come seeking fruit on this fig tree, and find none; cut it down; why cumbereth it the ground?" ⁸And he answering said unto him, "Lord, let it alone this year also, till I shall dig about it, and dung it; ⁹and if it bear fruit, well; and if not, then after that thou shalt cut it down."'

¹⁰And he was teaching in one of the synagogues on the sabbath. ¹¹And, behold, there was a woman which had a spirit of infirmity eighteen years, and was bowed together, and could in no wise lift up herself. ¹²And when Jesus saw her, he called her to him, and said unto her, 'Woman, thou art loosed from thine infirmity.' ¹³And he laid his hands on her: and immediately she was made straight, and glorified God. ¹⁴And the ruler of the synagogue answered with indignation, because that Jesus had healed on the sabbath day, and said unto the people, 'There are six days in which men ought to work; in them therefore come and be healed, and

not on the sabbath day.' ¹⁵ The Lord then answered him, and said, 'Thou hypocrite, doth not each one of you on the sabbath loose his ox or his ass from the stall, and lead him away to watering? ¹⁶ And ought not this woman, being a daughter of Abraham, whom Satan hath bound, lo, these eighteen years, be loosed from this bond on the sabbath day?' ¹⁷ And when he had said these things, all his adversaries were ashamed: and all the people rejoiced for all the glorious things that were done by him.

¹⁸ Then said he, 'Unto what is the kingdom of God like? And whereunto shall I resemble it? ¹⁹ It is like a grain of mustard seed, which a man took, and cast into his garden; and it grew, and waxed a great tree; and the fowls of the air lodged in the branches of it.' ²⁰ And again he said, 'Whereunto shall I liken the kingdom of God?' ²¹ It is like leaven, which a woman took and hid in three measures of meal, till the whole was leavened.'

²² And he went through the cities and villages, teaching, and journeying toward Jerusalem. ²³ Then said one unto him, 'Lord, are there few that be saved?' And he said unto them, ²⁴ 'Strive to enter in at the strait gate; for many, I say unto you, will seek to enter in, and shall not be able. ²⁵ When once the master of the house is risen up, and hath shut to the door, and ye begin to stand without, and to knock at the door, saying, "Lord, Lord, open unto us"; and he shall answer and say unto you, "I know you not whence ye are," ²⁶ then shall ye begin to say, "We have eaten and drunk in thy presence, and thou hast taught in our streets." ²⁷ But he shall say, "I tell you, I know you not whence ye are; depart from me, all ye workers of iniquity." ²⁸ There shall be weeping and

gnashing of teeth, when ye shall see Abraham, and Isaac, and Jacob, and all the prophets, in the kingdom of God, and you yourselves thrust out. ²⁹And they shall come from the east, and from the west, and from the north, and from the south, and shall sit down in the kingdom of God. ³⁰And, behold, there are last which shall be first, and there are first which shall be last.'

³¹The same day there came certain of the Pharisees, saying unto him, 'Get thee out, and depart hence; for Herod will kill thee.' ³²And he said unto them, 'Go ye, and tell that fox, "Behold, I cast out devils, and I do cures today and tomorrow, and the third day I shall be perfected. ³³Nevertheless I must walk today, and tomorrow, and the day following; for it cannot be that a prophet perish out of Jerusalem." ³⁴O Jerusalem, Jerusalem, which killest the prophets, and stonest them that are sent unto thee; how often would I have gathered thy children together, as a hen doth gather her brood under her wings, and ye would not! ³⁵Behold, your house is left unto you desolate: and verily I say unto you, ye shall not see me, until the time come when ye shall say, "Blessed is he that cometh in the name of the Lord."'

14 And it came to pass, as he went into the house of one of the chief Pharisees to eat bread on the sabbath day, that they watched him. ²And, behold, there was a certain man before him which had the dropsy. ³And Jesus answering spake unto the lawyers and Pharisees, saying, 'Is it lawful to heal on the sabbath day?' ⁴And they held their peace. And he took him, and healed him, and let him go; ⁵and answered them, saying, 'Which of you shall have an ass or

an ox fallen into a pit, and will not straightway pull him out on the sabbath day?' ⁶And they could not answer him again to these things.

⁷And he put forth a parable to those which were bidden, when he marked how they chose out the chief rooms; saying unto them, ⁸'When thou art bidden of any man to a wedding, sit not down in the highest room, lest a more honourable man than thou be bidden of him; ⁹and he that bade thee and him come and say to thee, "Give this man place"; and thou begin with shame to take the lowest room. ¹⁰But when thou art bidden, go and sit down in the lowest room; that when he that bade thee cometh, he may say unto thee, "Friend, go up higher," then shalt thou have worship in the presence of them that sit at meat with thee. ¹¹For whosoever exalteth himself shall be abased; and he that humbleth himself shall be exalted.'

¹²Then said he also to him that bade him, 'When thou makest a dinner or a supper, call not thy friends, nor thy brethren, neither thy kinsmen, nor thy rich neighbours, lest they also bid thee again, and a recompence be made thee. ¹³But when thou makest a feast, call the poor, the maimed, the lame, the blind; ¹⁴and thou shalt be blessed; for they cannot recompense thee; for thou shalt be recompensed at the resurrection of the just.'

¹⁵And when one of them that sat at meat with him heard these things, he said unto him, 'Blessed is he that shall eat bread in the kingdom of God.' ¹⁶Then said he unto him, 'A certain man made a great supper, and bade many, ¹⁷and sent his servant at supper time to say to them that were bidden, "Come; for all things are now ready." ¹⁸And they all with

one consent began to make excuse. The first said unto him, "I have bought a piece of ground, and I must needs go and see it: I pray thee have me excused." ¹⁹And another said, "I have bought five yoke of oxen, and I go to prove them: I pray thee have me excused." ²⁰And another said, "I have married a wife, and therefore I cannot come." ²¹So that servant came, and shewed his lord these things. Then the master of the house being angry said to his servant, "Go out quickly into the streets and lanes of the city, and bring in hither the poor, and the maimed, and the halt, and the blind." ²²And the servant said, "Lord, it is done as thou hast commanded, and yet there is room." ²³And the lord said unto the servant, "Go out into the highways and hedges, and compel them to come in, that my house may be filled. ²⁴For I say unto you that none of those men which were bidden shall taste of my supper."'

²⁵And there went great multitudes with him; and he turned, and said unto them, ²⁶'If any man come to me, and hate not his father, and mother, and wife, and children, and brethren, and sisters, yea, and his own life also, he cannot be my disciple. ²⁷And whosoever doth not bear his cross, and come after me, cannot be my disciple. ²⁸For which of you, intending to build a tower, sitteth not down first, and counteth the cost, whether he have sufficient to finish it? ²⁹Lest haply, after he hath laid the foundation, and is not able to finish it, all that behold it begin to mock him, ³⁰saying, "This man began to build, and was not able to finish." ³¹Or what king, going to make war against another king, sitteth not down first, and consulteth whether he be able with ten thousand to meet him that cometh against him with twenty thousand?

³² Or else, while the other is yet a great way off, he sendeth an ambassage, and desireth conditions of peace. ³³ So likewise, whosoever he be of you that forsaketh not all that he hath, he cannot be my disciple.

³⁴ 'Salt is good: but if the salt have lost his savour, wherewith shall it be seasoned? ³⁵ It is neither fit for the land, nor yet for the dunghill; but men cast it out. He that hath ears to hear, let him hear.'

15 Then drew near unto him all the publicans and sinners for to hear him. ²And the Pharisees and scribes murmured, saying, 'This man receiveth sinners, and eateth with them.'

³And he spake this parable unto them, saying, ⁴'What man of you, having an hundred sheep, if he lose one of them, doth not leave the ninety and nine in the wilderness, and go after that which is lost, until he find it? ⁵And when he hath found it, he layeth it on his shoulders, rejoicing. ⁶And when he cometh home, he calleth together his friends and neighbours, saying unto them, "Rejoice with me; for I have found my sheep which was lost." ⁷ I say unto you, that likewise joy shall be in heaven over one sinner that repenteth, more than over ninety and nine just persons, which need no repentance.

⁸ 'Either what woman having ten pieces of silver, if she lose one piece, doth not light a candle, and sweep the house, and seek diligently till she find it? ⁹And when she hath found it, she calleth her friends and her neighbours together, saying, "Rejoice with me; for I have found the piece which I had lost." ¹⁰Likewise, I say unto you, there is joy in the presence of the angels of God over one sinner that repenteth.'

[11]And he said, 'A certain man had two sons: [12]and the younger of them said to his father, "Father, give me the portion of goods that falleth to me." And he divided unto them his living. [13]And not many days after the younger son gathered all together, and took his journey into a far country, and there wasted his substance with riotous living. [14]And when he had spent all, there arose a mighty famine in that land; and he began to be in want. [15]And he went and joined himself to a citizen of that country; and he sent him into his fields to feed swine. [16]And he would fain have filled his belly with the husks that the swine did eat; and no man gave unto him. [17]And when he came to himself, he said, "How many hired servants of my father's have bread enough and to spare, and I perish with hunger! [18]I will arise and go to my father, and will say unto him, Father, I have sinned against heaven, and before thee, [19]and am no more worthy to be called thy son; make me as one of thy hired servants." [20]And he arose, and came to his father. But when he was yet a great way off, his father saw him, and had compassion, and ran, and fell on his neck, and kissed him. [21]And the son said unto him, "Father, I have sinned against heaven, and in thy sight, and am no more worthy to be called thy son." [22]But the father said to his servants, "Bring forth the best robe, and put it on him; and put a ring on his hand, and shoes on his feet: [23]and bring hither the fatted calf, and kill it; and let us eat, and be merry. [24]For this my son was dead, and is alive again; he was lost, and is found." And they began to be merry. [25]Now his elder son was in the field; and as he came and drew nigh to the house, he heard musick and dancing. [26]And he called one of the servants, and asked what these things meant. [27]And he

said unto him, "Thy brother is come; and thy father hath killed the fatted calf, because he hath received him safe and sound." ²⁸And he was angry, and would not go in; therefore came his father out, and intreated him. ²⁹And he answering said to his father, "Lo, these many years do I serve thee, neither transgressed I at any time thy commandment: and yet thou never gavest me a kid, that I might make merry with my friends. ³⁰But as soon as this thy son was come, which hath devoured thy living with harlots, thou hast killed for him the fatted calf." ³¹And he said unto him, "Son, thou art ever with me, and all that I have is thine. ³²It was meet that we should make merry, and be glad; for this thy brother was dead, and is alive again; and was lost, and is found."'

16 And he said also unto his disciples, 'There was a certain rich man, which had a steward; and the same was accused unto him that he had wasted his goods. ²And he called him, and said unto him, "How is it that I hear this of thee? Give an account of thy stewardship; for thou mayest be no longer steward." ³Then the steward said within himself, "What shall I do? For my lord taketh away from me the stewardship. I cannot dig; to beg I am ashamed. ⁴I am resolved what to do, that, when I am put out of the stewardship, they may receive me into their houses." ⁵So he called every one of his lord's debtors unto him, and said unto the first, "How much owest thou unto my lord?" ⁶And he said, "An hundred measures of oil." And he said unto him, "Take thy bill, and sit down quickly, and write fifty." ⁷Then said he to another, "And how much owest thou?" And he said, "An hundred measures of wheat." And he said unto him, "Take

thy bill, and write fourscore." [8] And the lord commended the unjust steward, because he had done wisely: for the children of this world are in their generation wiser than the children of light. [9] And I say unto you, make to yourselves friends of the mammon of unrighteousness; that, when ye fail, they may receive you into everlasting habitations.

[10] 'He that is faithful in that which is least is faithful also in much: and he that is unjust in the least is unjust also in much. [11] If therefore ye have not been faithful in the unrighteous mammon, who will commit to your trust the true riches? [12] And if ye have not been faithful in that which is another man's, who shall give you that which is your own?

[13] 'No servant can serve two masters: for either he will hate the one, and love the other; or else he will hold to the one, and despise the other. Ye cannot serve God and mammon.'

[14] And the Pharisees also, who were covetous, heard all these things: and they derided him. [15] And he said unto them, 'Ye are they which justify yourselves before men, but God knoweth your hearts, for that which is highly esteemed among men is abomination in the sight of God. [16] The law and the prophets were until John; since that time the kingdom of God is preached, and every man presseth into it. [17] And it is easier for heaven and earth to pass, than one tittle of the law to fail. [18] Whosoever putteth away his wife, and marrieth another, committeth adultery; and whosoever marrieth her that is put away from her husband committeth adultery.

[19] 'There was a certain rich man, which was clothed in purple and fine linen, and fared sumptuously every day; [20] and there was a certain beggar named Lazarus, which was laid at his gate, full of sores, [21] and desiring to be fed with the

crumbs which fell from the rich man's table; moreover the dogs came and licked his sores. ²²And it came to pass that the beggar died, and was carried by the angels into Abraham's bosom; the rich man also died, and was buried; ²³and in hell he lift up his eyes, being in torments, and seeth Abraham afar off, and Lazarus in his bosom. ²⁴And he cried and said, "Father Abraham, have mercy on me, and send Lazarus that he may dip the tip of his finger in water, and cool my tongue; for I am tormented in this flame." ²⁵But Abraham said, "Son, remember that thou in thy lifetime receivedst thy good things, and likewise Lazarus evil things; but now he is comforted, and thou art tormented. ²⁶And beside all this, between us and you there is a great gulf fixed: so that they which would pass from hence to you cannot; neither can they pass to us, that would come from thence." ²⁷Then he said, "I pray thee therefore, father, that thou wouldest send him to my father's house, ²⁸for I have five brethren; that he may testify unto them, lest they also come into this place of torment." ²⁹Abraham saith unto him, "They have Moses and the prophets; let them hear them." ³⁰And he said, "Nay, father Abraham: but if one went unto them from the dead, they will repent." ³¹And he said unto him, "If they hear not Moses and the prophets, neither will they be persuaded, though one rose from the dead."'

17 Then said he unto the disciples, 'It is impossible but that offences will come: but woe unto him, through whom they come! ²It were better for him that a millstone were hanged about his neck, and he cast into the sea, than that he should offend one of these little ones.

³ 'Take heed to yourselves: if thy brother trespass against thee, rebuke him; and if he repent, forgive him. ⁴And if he trespass against thee seven times in a day, and seven times in a day turn again to thee, saying, "I repent," thou shalt forgive him.'

⁵And the apostles said unto the Lord, 'Increase our faith.' ⁶And the Lord said, 'If ye had faith as a grain of mustard seed, ye might say unto this sycamine tree, "Be thou plucked up by the root, and be thou planted in the sea"; and it should obey you. ⁷But which of you, having a servant plowing or feeding cattle, will say unto him by and by, when he is come from the field, "Go and sit down to meat"? ⁸And will not rather say unto him, "Make ready wherewith I may sup, and gird thyself, and serve me, till I have eaten and drunken; and afterward thou shalt eat and drink"? ⁹Doth he thank that servant because he did the things that were commanded him? I trow not. ¹⁰So likewise ye, when ye shall have done all those things which are commanded you, say, "We are unprofitable servants: we have done that which was our duty to do."'

¹¹And it came to pass, as he went to Jerusalem, that he passed through the midst of Samaria and Galilee. ¹²And as he entered into a certain village, there met him ten men that were lepers, which stood afar off. ¹³And they lifted up their voices, and said, 'Jesus, Master, have mercy on us.' ¹⁴And when he saw them, he said unto them, 'Go shew yourselves unto the priests.' And it came to pass, that, as they went, they were cleansed. ¹⁵And one of them, when he saw that he was healed, turned back, and with a loud voice glorified God, ¹⁶and fell down on his face at his feet, giving him thanks; and he was a Samaritan. ¹⁷And Jesus answering said,

'Were there not ten cleansed? But where are the nine? [18] There are not found that returned to give glory to God, save this stranger.' [19] And he said unto him, 'Arise, go thy way; thy faith hath made thee whole.'

[20] And when he was demanded of the Pharisees, when the kingdom of God should come, he answered them and said, 'The kingdom of God cometh not with observation. [21] Neither shall they say, "Lo here!" or, "Lo there!" For, behold, the kingdom of God is within you.' [22] And he said unto the disciples, 'The days will come, when ye shall desire to see one of the days of the Son of man, and ye shall not see it. [23] And they shall say to you, "See here," or, "See there": go not after them, nor follow them. [24] For as the lightning, that lighteneth out of the one part under heaven, shineth unto the other part under heaven; so shall also the Son of man be in his day. [25] But first must he suffer many things, and be rejected of this generation. [26] And as it was in the days of Noe, so shall it be also in the days of the Son of man. [27] They did eat, they drank, they married wives, they were given in marriage, until the day that Noe entered into the ark, and the flood came, and destroyed them all. [28] Likewise also as it was in the days of Lot; they did eat, they drank, they bought, they sold, they planted, they builded; [29] but the same day that Lot went out of Sodom it rained fire and brimstone from heaven, and destroyed them all. [30] Even thus shall it be in the day when the Son of man is revealed. [31] In that day, he which shall be upon the housetop, and his stuff in the house, let him not come down to take it away; and he that is in the field, let him likewise not return back. [32] Remember Lot's wife. [33] Whosoever shall seek to save his life shall lose it; and

whosoever shall lose his life shall preserve it. ³⁴ I tell you, in that night there shall be two men in one bed; the one shall be taken, and the other shall be left. ³⁵ Two women shall be grinding together; the one shall be taken, and the other left. ³⁶ Two men shall be in the field; the one shall be taken, and the other left.' ³⁷ And they answered and said unto him, 'Where, Lord?' And he said unto them, 'Wheresoever the body is, thither will the eagles be gathered together.'

18 And he spake a parable unto them to this end, that men ought always to pray, and not to faint; ² saying, 'There was in a city a judge, which feared not God, neither regarded man; ³ and there was a widow in that city; and she came unto him, saying, "Avenge me of mine adversary." ⁴ And he would not for a while; but afterward he said within himself, "Though I fear not God, nor regard man; ⁵ yet because this widow troubleth me, I will avenge her, lest by her continual coming she weary me."' ⁶ And the Lord said, 'Hear what the unjust judge saith. ⁷ And shall not God avenge his own elect, which cry day and night unto him, though he bear long with them? ⁸ I tell you that he will avenge them speedily. Nevertheless when the Son of man cometh, shall he find faith on the earth?'

⁹ And he spake this parable unto certain which trusted in themselves that they were righteous, and despised others. ¹⁰ 'Two men went up into the temple to pray: the one a Pharisee, and the other a publican. ¹¹ The Pharisee stood and prayed thus with himself, "God, I thank thee, that I am not as other men are, extortioners, unjust, adulterers, or even as this publican. ¹² I fast twice in the week, I give tithes of all that I possess."

¹³And the publican, standing afar off, would not lift up so much as his eyes unto heaven, but smote upon his breast, saying, "God be merciful to me a sinner." ¹⁴I tell you, this man went down to his house justified rather than the other: for every one that exalteth himself shall be abased; and he that humbleth himself shall be exalted.'

¹⁵And they brought unto him also infants, that he would touch them; but when his disciples saw it, they rebuked them. ¹⁶But Jesus called them unto him, and said, 'Suffer little children to come unto me, and forbid them not; for of such is the kingdom of God. ¹⁷Verily I say unto you, whosoever shall not receive the kingdom of God as a little child shall in no wise enter therein.'

¹⁸And a certain ruler asked him, saying, 'Good Master, what shall I do to inherit eternal life?' ¹⁹And Jesus said unto him, 'Why callest thou me good? None is good, save one, that is, God. ²⁰Thou knowest the commandments: Do not commit adultery, Do not kill, Do not steal, Do not bear false witness, Honour thy father and thy mother.' ²¹And he said, 'All these have I kept from my youth up.' ²²Now when Jesus heard these things, he said unto him, 'Yet lackest thou one thing: sell all that thou hast, and distribute unto the poor, and thou shalt have treasure in heaven; and come, follow me.' ²³And when he heard this, he was very sorrowful; for he was very rich. ²⁴And when Jesus saw that he was very sorrowful, he said, 'How hardly shall they that have riches enter into the kingdom of God! ²⁵For it is easier for a camel to go through a needle's eye, than for a rich man to enter into the kingdom of God.' ²⁶And they that heard it said, 'Who then can be saved?' ²⁷And he said, 'The things which are impossible with men

are possible with God.' ²⁸Then Peter said, 'Lo, we have left all, and followed thee.' ²⁹And he said unto them, 'Verily I say unto you, there is no man that hath left house, or parents, or brethren, or wife, or children, for the kingdom of God's sake, ³⁰ who shall not receive manifold more in this present time, and in the world to come life everlasting.'

³¹Then he took unto him the twelve, and said unto them, 'Behold, we go up to Jerusalem, and all things that are written by the prophets concerning the Son of man shall be accomplished. ³²For he shall be delivered unto the Gentiles, and shall be mocked, and spitefully entreated, and spitted on. ³³And they shall scourge him, and put him to death; and the third day he shall rise again.' ³⁴And they understood none of these things; and this saying was hid from them, neither knew they the things which were spoken.

³⁵And it came to pass that, as he was come nigh unto Jericho, a certain blind man sat by the way side begging, ³⁶and hearing the multitude pass by, he asked what it meant. ³⁷And they told him that Jesus of Nazareth passeth by. ³⁸And he cried, saying, 'Jesus, thou Son of David, have mercy on me.' ³⁹And they which went before rebuked him, that he should hold his peace: but he cried so much the more, 'Thou Son of David, have mercy on me.' ⁴⁰And Jesus stood, and commanded him to be brought unto him; and when he was come near, he asked him, ⁴¹saying, 'What wilt thou that I shall do unto thee?' And he said, 'Lord, that I may receive my sight.' ⁴²And Jesus said unto him, 'Receive thy sight; thy faith hath saved thee.' ⁴³And immediately he received his sight, and followed him, glorifying God: and all the people, when they saw it, gave praise unto God.

19 And Jesus entered and passed through Jericho. ²And, behold, there was a man named Zacchæus, which was the chief among the publicans, and he was rich. ³And he sought to see Jesus who he was; and could not for the press, because he was little of stature. ⁴And he ran before, and climbed up into a sycomore tree to see him; for he was to pass that way. ⁵And when Jesus came to the place, he looked up, and saw him, and said unto him, 'Zacchæus, make haste, and come down; for today I must abide at thy house.' ⁶And he made haste, and came down, and received him joyfully. ⁷And when they saw it, they all murmured, saying that he was gone to be guest with a man that is a sinner. ⁸And Zacchæus stood, and said unto the Lord, 'Behold, Lord, the half of my goods I give to the poor; and if I have taken any thing from any man by false accusation, I restore him fourfold.' ⁹And Jesus said unto him, 'This day is salvation come to this house, forsomuch as he also is a son of Abraham. ¹⁰For the Son of man is come to seek and to save that which was lost.'

¹¹And as they heard these things, he added and spake a parable, because he was nigh to Jerusalem, and because they thought that the kingdom of God should immediately appear. ¹²He said therefore, 'A certain nobleman went into a far country to receive for himself a kingdom, and to return. ¹³And he called his ten servants, and delivered them ten pounds, and said unto them, "Occupy till I come." ¹⁴But his citizens hated him, and sent a message after him, saying, "We will not have this man to reign over us." ¹⁵And it came to pass that, when he was returned, having received the kingdom, then he commanded these servants to be called unto him, to whom he had given the money, that he might know

how much every man had gained by trading. ¹⁶Then came the first, saying, "Lord, thy pound hath gained ten pounds." ¹⁷And he said unto him, "Well, thou good servant, because thou hast been faithful in a very little, have thou authority over ten cities." ¹⁸And the second came, saying, "Lord, thy pound hath gained five pounds." ¹⁹And he said likewise to him, "Be thou also over five cities." ²⁰And another came, saying, "Lord, behold, here is thy pound, which I have kept laid up in a napkin; ²¹for I feared thee, because thou art an austere man: thou takest up that thou layedst not down, and reapest that thou didst not sow." ²²And he saith unto him, "Out of thine own mouth will I judge thee, thou wicked servant. Thou knewest that I was an austere man, taking up that I laid not down, and reaping that I did not sow. ²³Wherefore then gavest not thou my money into the bank, that at my coming I might have required mine own with usury?" ²⁴And he said unto them that stood by, "Take from him the pound, and give it to him that hath ten pounds." ²⁵(And they said unto him, "Lord, he hath ten pounds.") ²⁶For I say unto you that unto every one which hath shall be given; and from him that hath not, even that he hath shall be taken away from him. ²⁷But those mine enemies, which would not that I should reign over them, bring hither, and slay them before me.'

²⁸And when he had thus spoken, he went before, ascending up to Jerusalem. ²⁹And it came to pass, when he was come nigh to Bethphage and Bethany, at the mount called the mount of Olives, he sent two of his disciples, ³⁰saying, 'Go ye into the village over against you, in the which at your entering ye shall find a colt tied, whereon yet never man sat: loose him, and bring him hither. ³¹And if any man ask you,

"Why do ye loose him?" Thus shall ye say unto him, "Because the Lord hath need of him."' ³²And they that were sent went their way, and found even as he had said unto them. ³³And as they were loosing the colt, the owners thereof said unto them, 'Why loose ye the colt?' ³⁴And they said, 'The Lord hath need of him.' ³⁵And they brought him to Jesus: and they cast their garments upon the colt, and they set Jesus thereon. ³⁶And as he went, they spread their clothes in the way. ³⁷And when he was come nigh, even now at the descent of the mount of Olives, the whole multitude of the disciples began to rejoice and praise God with a loud voice for all the mighty works that they had seen, ³⁸saying, 'Blessed be the King that cometh in the name of the Lord; peace in heaven, and glory in the highest.' ³⁹And some of the Pharisees from among the multitude said unto him, 'Master, rebuke thy disciples.' ⁴⁰And he answered and said unto them, 'I tell you that, if these should hold their peace, the stones would immediately cry out.'

⁴¹And when he was come near, he beheld the city, and wept over it, ⁴²saying, 'If thou hadst known, even thou, at least in this thy day, the things which belong unto thy peace! But now they are hid from thine eyes. ⁴³For the days shall come upon thee, that thine enemies shall cast a trench about thee, and compass thee round, and keep thee in on every side, ⁴⁴and shall lay thee even with the ground, and thy children within thee; and they shall not leave in thee one stone upon another; because thou knewest not the time of thy visitation.' ⁴⁵And he went into the temple, and began to cast out them that sold therein, and them that bought, ⁴⁶saying unto them, 'It is written, "My house is the house of prayer," but ye have

made it a den of thieves.' ⁴⁷And he taught daily in the temple. But the chief priests and the scribes and the chief of the people sought to destroy him, ⁴⁸and could not find what they might do; for all the people were very attentive to hear him.

20 And it came to pass that on one of those days, as he taught the people in the temple, and preached the gospel, the chief priests and the scribes came upon him with the elders, ²and spake unto him, saying, 'Tell us, by what authority doest thou these things? Or who is he that gave thee this authority?' ³And he answered and said unto them, 'I will also ask you one thing; and answer me: ⁴the baptism of John, was it from heaven, or of men?' ⁵And they reasoned with themselves, saying, 'If we shall say, "From heaven," he will say, "Why then believed ye him not?"; ⁶but and if we say, "Of men; all the people will stone us; for they be persuaded that John was a prophet.' ⁷And they answered that they could not tell whence it was. ⁸And Jesus said unto them, 'Neither tell I you by what authority I do these things.'

⁹Then began he to speak to the people this parable: 'A certain man planted a vineyard, and let it forth to husbandmen, and went into a far country for a long time. ¹⁰And at the season he sent a servant to the husbandmen, that they should give him of the fruit of the vineyard; but the husbandmen beat him, and sent him away empty. ¹¹And again he sent another servant: and they beat him also, and entreated him shamefully, and sent him away empty. ¹²And again he sent a third; and they wounded him also, and cast him out. ¹³Then said the lord of the vineyard, "What shall I do? I will send my beloved son; it may be they will reverence him when

they see him." ¹⁴ But when the husbandmen saw him, they reasoned among themselves, saying, "This is the heir: come, let us kill him, that the inheritance may be ours." ¹⁵ So they cast him out of the vineyard, and killed him. What therefore shall the lord of the vineyard do unto them? ¹⁶ He shall come and destroy these husbandmen, and shall give the vineyard to others.' And when they heard it, they said, 'God forbid.' ¹⁷ And he beheld them, and said, 'What is this then that is written, "The stone which the builders rejected, the same is become the head of the corner"? ¹⁸ Whosoever shall fall upon that stone shall be broken; but on whomsoever it shall fall, it will grind him to powder.'

¹⁹ And the chief priests and the scribes the same hour sought to lay hands on him; and they feared the people; for they perceived that he had spoken this parable against them. ²⁰ And they watched him, and sent forth spies, which should feign themselves just men, that they might take hold of his words, that so they might deliver him unto the power and authority of the governor. ²¹ And they asked him, saying, 'Master, we know that thou sayest and teachest rightly, neither acceptest thou the person of any, but teachest the way of God truly. ²² Is it lawful for us to give tribute unto Cæsar, or no?' ²³ But he perceived their craftiness, and said unto them, 'Why tempt ye me? ²⁴ Shew me a penny. Whose image and superscription hath it?' They answered and said, 'Cæsar's.' ²⁵ And he said unto them, 'Render therefore unto Cæsar the things which be Cæsar's, and unto God the things which be God's.' ²⁶ And they could not take hold of his words before the people: and they marvelled at his answer, and held their peace.

²⁷ Then came to him certain of the Sadducees, which deny

that there is any resurrection; and they asked him, ²⁸ saying, 'Master, Moses wrote unto us, if any man's brother die, having a wife, and he die without children, that his brother should take his wife, and raise up seed unto his brother. ²⁹ There were therefore seven brethren; and the first took a wife, and died without children. ³⁰ And the second took her to wife, and he died childless. ³¹ And the third took her; and in like manner the seven also: and they left no children, and died. ³² Last of all the woman died also. ³³ Therefore in the resurrection whose wife of them is she? For seven had her to wife.' ³⁴ And Jesus answering said unto them, 'The children of this world marry, and are given in marriage, ³⁵ but they which shall be accounted worthy to obtain that world, and the resurrection from the dead, neither marry, nor are given in marriage; ³⁶ neither can they die any more: for they are equal unto the angels; and are the children of God, being the children of the resurrection. ³⁷ Now that the dead are raised, even Moses shewed at the bush, when he calleth the Lord the God of Abraham, and the God of Isaac, and the God of Jacob. ³⁸ For he is not a God of the dead, but of the living: for all live unto him.'

³⁹ Then certain of the scribes answering said, 'Master, thou hast well said.' ⁴⁰ And after that they durst not ask him any question at all. ⁴¹ And he said unto them, 'How say they that Christ is David's son? ⁴² And David himself saith in the book of Psalms, "The Lord said unto my Lord, 'Sit thou on my right hand, ⁴³ till I make thine enemies thy footstool." ⁴⁴ David therefore calleth him Lord, how is he then his son?'

⁴⁵ Then in the audience of all the people he said unto his disciples, ⁴⁶ 'Beware of the scribes, which desire to walk in long robes, and love greetings in the markets, and the

highest seats in the synagogues, and the chief rooms at feasts; [47] which devour widows' houses, and for a shew make long prayers: the same shall receive greater damnation.'

21 And he looked up, and saw the rich men casting their gifts into the treasury. [2] And he saw also a certain poor widow casting in thither two mites. [3] And he said, 'Of a truth I say unto you that this poor widow hath cast in more than they all. [4] For all these have of their abundance cast in unto the offerings of God, but she of her penury hath cast in all the living that she had.'

[5] And as some spake of the temple, how it was adorned with goodly stones and gifts, he said, [6] 'As for these things which ye behold, the days will come, in the which there shall not be left one stone upon another, that shall not be thrown down.' [7] And they asked him, saying, 'Master, but when shall these things be? And what sign will there be when these things shall come to pass?' [8] And he said, 'Take heed that ye be not deceived; for many shall come in my name, saying, "I am Christ," and the time draweth near: go ye not therefore after them.

[9] 'But when ye shall hear of wars and commotions, be not terrified; for these things must first come to pass, but the end is not by and by.' [10] Then said he unto them, 'Nation shall rise against nation, and kingdom against kingdom. [11] And great earthquakes shall be in divers places, and famines, and pestilences; and fearful sights and great signs shall there be from heaven.

[12] 'But before all these, they shall lay their hands on you, and persecute you, delivering you up to the synagogues, and

into prisons, being brought before kings and rulers for my name's sake. ¹³And it shall turn to you for a testimony. ¹⁴Settle it therefore in your hearts, not to meditate before what ye shall answer, ¹⁵for I will give you a mouth and wisdom, which all your adversaries shall not be able to gainsay nor resist. ¹⁶And ye shall be betrayed both by parents, and brethren, and kinsfolks, and friends; and some of you shall they cause to be put to death. ¹⁷And ye shall be hated of all men for my name's sake. ¹⁸But there shall not an hair of your head perish. ¹⁹In your patience possess ye your souls. ²⁰And when ye shall see Jerusalem compassed with armies, then know that the desolation thereof is nigh. ²¹Then let them which are in Judæa flee to the mountains; and let them which are in the midst of it depart out; and let not them that are in the countries enter thereinto. ²²For these be the days of vengeance, that all things which are written may be fulfilled. ²³But woe unto them that are with child, and to them that give suck, in those days! For there shall be great distress in the land, and wrath upon this people. ²⁴And they shall fall by the edge of the sword, and shall be led away captive into all nations: and Jerusalem shall be trodden down of the Gentiles, until the times of the Gentiles be fulfilled.

²⁵'And there shall be signs in the sun, and in the moon, and in the stars; and upon the earth distress of nations, with perplexity; the sea and the waves roaring; ²⁶men's hearts failing them for fear, and for looking after those things which are coming on the earth: for the powers of heaven shall be shaken. ²⁷And then shall they see the Son of man coming in a cloud with power and great glory. ²⁸And when these things begin to come to pass, then look up, and lift up your heads;

for your redemption draweth nigh.' ²⁹And he spake to them a parable: 'Behold the fig tree, and all the trees; ³⁰when they now shoot forth, ye see and know of your own selves that summer is now nigh at hand. ³¹So likewise ye, when ye see these things come to pass, know ye that the kingdom of God is nigh at hand. ³²Verily I say unto you, this generation shall not pass away, till all be fulfilled. ³³Heaven and earth shall pass away, but my words shall not pass away.

³⁴And take heed to yourselves, lest at any time your hearts be overcharged with surfeiting, and drunkenness, and cares of this life, and so that day come upon you unawares. ³⁵For as a snare shall it come on all them that dwell on the face of the whole earth. ³⁶Watch ye therefore, and pray always, that ye may be accounted worthy to escape all these things that shall come to pass, and to stand before the Son of man.' ³⁷And in the day time he was teaching in the temple; and at night he went out, and abode in the mount that is called the mount of Olives. ³⁸And all the people came early in the morning to him in the temple, for to hear him.

22 Now the feast of unleavened bread drew nigh, which is called the Passover. ²And the chief priests and scribes sought how they might kill him; for they feared the people.

³Then entered Satan into Judas surnamed Iscariot, being of the number of the twelve. ⁴And he went his way, and communed with the chief priests and captains, how he might betray him unto them. ⁵And they were glad, and covenanted to give him money. ⁶And he promised, and sought opportunity to betray him unto them in the absence of the multitude.

⁷ Then came the day of unleavened bread, when the passover must be killed. ⁸ And he sent Peter and John, saying, 'Go and prepare us the passover, that we may eat.' ⁹ And they said unto him, 'Where wilt thou that we prepare?' ¹⁰ And he said unto them, 'Behold, when ye are entered into the city, there shall a man meet you, bearing a pitcher of water; follow him into the house where he entereth in. ¹¹ And ye shall say unto the goodman of the house, "The Master saith unto thee, 'Where is the guestchamber, where I shall eat the passover with my disciples?'" ¹² And he shall shew you a large upper room furnished; there make ready.' ¹³ And they went, and found as he had said unto them: and they made ready the passover.

¹⁴ And when the hour was come, he sat down, and the twelve apostles with him. ¹⁵ And he said unto them, 'With desire I have desired to eat this passover with you before I suffer. ¹⁶ For I say unto you, I will not any more eat thereof, until it be fulfilled in the kingdom of God.' ¹⁷ And he took the cup, and gave thanks, and said, 'Take this, and divide it among yourselves. ¹⁸ For I say unto you, I will not drink of the fruit of the vine, until the kingdom of God shall come.'

¹⁹ And he took bread, and gave thanks, and brake it, and gave unto them, saying, 'This is my body which is given for you: this do in remembrance of me.' ²⁰ Likewise also the cup after supper, saying, 'This cup is the new testament in my blood, which is shed for you. ²¹ But, behold, the hand of him that betrayeth me is with me on the table. ²² And truly the Son of man goeth, as it was determined: but woe unto that man by whom he is betrayed!' ²³ And they began to enquire among themselves, which of them it was that should do this thing.

²⁴And there was also a strife among them, which of them should be accounted the greatest. ²⁵And he said unto them, 'The kings of the Gentiles exercise lordship over them; and they that exercise authority upon them are called benefactors. ²⁶But ye shall not be so: but he that is greatest among you, let him be as the younger; and he that is chief, as he that doth serve. ²⁷For whether is greater, he that sitteth at meat, or he that serveth? Is not he that sitteth at meat? But I am among you as he that serveth. ²⁸Ye are they which have continued with me in my temptations. ²⁹And I appoint unto you a kingdom, as my Father hath appointed unto me; ³⁰that ye may eat and drink at my table in my kingdom, and sit on thrones judging the twelve tribes of Israel.'

³¹And the Lord said, 'Simon, Simon, behold, Satan hath desired to have you, that he may sift you as wheat; ³²but I have prayed for thee, that thy faith fail not; and when thou art converted, strengthen thy brethren.' ³³And he said unto him, 'Lord, I am ready to go with thee, both into prison, and to death.' ³⁴And he said, 'I tell thee, Peter, the cock shall not crow this day, before that thou shalt thrice deny that thou knowest me.' ³⁵And he said unto them, 'When I sent you without purse, and scrip, and shoes, lacked ye any thing?' And they said, 'Nothing.' ³⁶Then said he unto them, 'But now, he that hath a purse, let him take it, and likewise his scrip: and he that hath no sword, let him sell his garment, and buy one. ³⁷For I say unto you that this that is written must yet be accomplished in me, and he was reckoned among the transgressors: for the things concerning me have an end.' ³⁸And they said, 'Lord, behold, here are two swords.' And he said unto them, 'It is enough.'

³⁹And he came out, and went, as he was wont, to the mount of Olives; and his disciples also followed him. ⁴⁰And when he was at the place, he said unto them, 'Pray that ye enter not into temptation.' ⁴¹And he was withdrawn from them about a stone's cast, and kneeled down, and prayed, ⁴²saying, 'Father, if thou be willing, remove this cup from me; nevertheless not my will, but thine, be done.' ⁴³And there appeared an angel unto him from heaven, strengthening him. ⁴⁴And being in an agony he prayed more earnestly; and his sweat was as it were great drops of blood falling down to the ground. ⁴⁵And when he rose up from prayer, and was come to his disciples, he found them sleeping for sorrow, ⁴⁶and said unto them, 'Why sleep ye? Rise and pray, lest ye enter into temptation.'

⁴⁷And while he yet spake, behold a multitude, and he that was called Judas, one of the twelve, went before them, and drew near unto Jesus to kiss him. ⁴⁸But Jesus said unto him, 'Judas, betrayest thou the Son of man with a kiss?' ⁴⁹When they which were about him saw what would follow, they said unto him, 'Lord, shall we smite with the sword?'

⁵⁰And one of them smote the servant of the high priest, and cut off his right ear. ⁵¹And Jesus answered and said, 'Suffer ye thus far.' And he touched his ear, and healed him. ⁵²Then Jesus said unto the chief priests, and captains of the temple, and the elders, which were come to him, 'Be ye come out, as against a thief, with swords and staves? ⁵³When I was daily with you in the temple, ye stretched forth no hands against me: but this is your hour, and the power of darkness.'

⁵⁴Then took they him, and led him, and brought him into the high priest's house. And Peter followed afar off. ⁵⁵And

when they had kindled a fire in the midst of the hall, and were set down together, Peter sat down among them. ⁵⁶ But a certain maid beheld him as he sat by the fire, and earnestly looked upon him, and said, 'This man was also with him.' ⁵⁷And he denied him, saying, 'Woman, I know him not.' ⁵⁸And after a little while another saw him, and said, 'Thou art also of them.' And Peter said, 'Man, I am not.' ⁵⁹And about the space of one hour after another confidently affirmed, saying, 'Of a truth this fellow also was with him; for he is a Galilæan.' ⁶⁰And Peter said, 'Man, I know not what thou sayest.' And immediately, while he yet spake, the cock crew. ⁶¹And the Lord turned, and looked upon Peter. And Peter remembered the word of the Lord, how he had said unto him, 'Before the cock crow, thou shalt deny me thrice.' ⁶²And Peter went out, and wept bitterly.

⁶³And the men that held Jesus mocked him, and smote him. ⁶⁴And when they had blindfolded him, they struck him on the face, and asked him, saying, 'Prophesy, who is it that smote thee?' ⁶⁵And many other things blasphemously spake they against him.

⁶⁶And as soon as it was day, the elders of the people and the chief priests and the scribes came together, and led him into their council, saying, ⁶⁷'Art thou the Christ? Tell us.' And he said unto them, 'If I tell you, ye will not believe. ⁶⁸And if I also ask you, ye will not answer me, nor let me go. ⁶⁹Hereafter shall the Son of man sit on the right hand of the power of God.' ⁷⁰Then said they all, 'Art thou then the Son of God?' And he said unto them, 'Ye say that I am.' ⁷¹And they said, 'What need we any further witness? For we ourselves have heard of his own mouth.'

23 And the whole multitude of them arose, and led him unto Pilate. ²And they began to accuse him, saying, 'We found this fellow perverting the nation, and forbidding to give tribute to Cæsar, saying that he himself is Christ a King.' ³And Pilate asked him, saying, 'Art thou the King of the Jews?' And he answered him and said, 'Thou sayest it.' ⁴Then said Pilate to the chief priests and to the people, 'I find no fault in this man.' ⁵And they were the more fierce, saying, 'He stirreth up the people, teaching throughout all Jewry, beginning from Galilee to this place.' ⁶When Pilate heard of Galilee, he asked whether the man were a Galilæan. ⁷And as soon as he knew that he belonged unto Herod's jurisdiction, he sent him to Herod, who himself also was at Jerusalem at that time.

⁸And when Herod saw Jesus, he was exceeding glad, for he was desirous to see him of a long season, because he had heard many things of him; and he hoped to have seen some miracle done by him. ⁹Then he questioned with him in many words; but he answered him nothing. ¹⁰And the chief priests and scribes stood and vehemently accused him. ¹¹And Herod with his men of war set him at nought, and mocked him, and arrayed him in a gorgeous robe, and sent him again to Pilate.

¹²And the same day Pilate and Herod were made friends together; for before they were at enmity between themselves.

¹³And Pilate, when he had called together the chief priests and the rulers and the people, ¹⁴said unto them, 'Ye have brought this man unto me, as one that perverteth the people: and, behold, I, having examined him before you, have found no fault in this man touching those things whereof ye accuse

him. ¹⁵ No, nor yet Herod: for I sent you to him; and, lo, nothing worthy of death is done unto him. ¹⁶ I will therefore chastise him, and release him.' ¹⁷(For of necessity he must release one unto them at the feast.)

¹⁸And they cried out all at once, saying, 'Away with this man, and release unto us Barabbas' ¹⁹(who for a certain sedition made in the city, and for murder, was cast into prison). ²⁰ Pilate therefore, willing to release Jesus, spake again to them. ²¹ But they cried, saying, 'Crucify him, crucify him.' ²²And he said unto them the third time, 'Why, what evil hath he done? I have found no cause of death in him: I will therefore chastise him, and let him go.' ²³And they were instant with loud voices, requiring that he might be crucified. And the voices of them and of the chief priests prevailed. ²⁴And Pilate gave sentence that it should be as they required. ²⁵And he released unto them him that for sedition and murder was cast into prison, whom they had desired; but he delivered Jesus to their will. ²⁶And as they led him away, they laid hold upon one Simon, a Cyrenian, coming out of the country, and on him they laid the cross, that he might bear it after Jesus.

²⁷And there followed him a great company of people, and of women, which also bewailed and lamented him. ²⁸ But Jesus turning unto them said, 'Daughters of Jerusalem, weep not for me, but weep for yourselves, and for your children. ²⁹ For, behold, the days are coming, in the which they shall say, "Blessed are the barren, and the wombs that never bore, and the paps which never gave suck." ³⁰ Then shall they begin to say to the mountains, "Fall on us," and to the hills, "Cover us." ³¹ For if they do these things in a green tree, what shall be done in the dry?' ³²And there were also two

other, malefactors, led with him to be put to death. ³³And when they were come to the place, which is called Calvary, there they crucified him, and the malefactors, one on the right hand, and the other on the left.

³⁴Then said Jesus, 'Father, forgive them; for they know not what they do.' And they parted his raiment, and cast lots. ³⁵And the people stood beholding. And the rulers also with them derided him, saying, 'He saved others; let him save himself, if he be Christ, the chosen of God.' ³⁶And the soldiers also mocked him, coming to him, and offering him vinegar, ³⁷and saying, 'If thou be the king of the Jews, save thyself.' ³⁸And a superscription also was written over him in letters of Greek, and Latin, and Hebrew, 'THIS IS THE KING OF THE JEWS.'

³⁹And one of the malefactors which were hanged railed on him, saying, 'If thou be Christ, save thyself and us.' ⁴⁰But the other answering rebuked him, saying, 'Dost not thou fear God, seeing thou art in the same condemnation? ⁴¹And we indeed justly; for we receive the due reward of our deeds: but this man hath done nothing amiss.' ⁴²And he said unto Jesus, 'Lord, remember me when thou comest into thy kingdom.' ⁴³And Jesus said unto him, 'Verily I say unto thee, today shalt thou be with me in paradise.'

⁴⁴And it was about the sixth hour, and there was a darkness over all the earth until the ninth hour. ⁴⁵And the sun was darkened, and the veil of the temple was rent in the midst.

⁴⁶And when Jesus had cried with a loud voice, he said, 'Father, into thy hands I commend my spirit,' and having said thus, he gave up the ghost. ⁴⁷Now when the centurion saw what was done, he glorified God, saying, 'Certainly this

was a righteous man.' ⁴⁸And all the people that came together to that sight, beholding the things which were done, smote their breasts, and returned. ⁴⁹And all his acquaintance, and the women that followed him from Galilee, stood afar off, beholding these things.

⁵⁰And, behold, there was a man named Joseph, a counsellor; and he was a good man, and a just. ⁵¹(The same had not consented to the counsel and deed of them.) He was of Arimathæa, a city of the Jews, who also himself waited for the kingdom of God. ⁵²This man went unto Pilate, and begged the body of Jesus. ⁵³And he took it down, and wrapped it in linen, and laid it in a sepulchre that was hewn in stone, wherein never man before was laid. ⁵⁴And that day was the preparation, and the sabbath drew on. ⁵⁵And the women also, which came with him from Galilee, followed after, and beheld the sepulchre, and how his body was laid. ⁵⁶And they returned, and prepared spices and ointments; and rested the sabbath day according to the commandment.

24 Now upon the first day of the week, very early in the morning, they came unto the sepulchre, bringing the spices which they had prepared, and certain others with them. ²And they found the stone rolled away from the sepulchre. ³And they entered in, and found not the body of the Lord Jesus. ⁴And it came to pass, as they were much perplexed thereabout, behold, two men stood by them in shining garments. ⁵And as they were afraid, and bowed down their faces to the earth, they said unto them, 'Why seek ye the living among the dead? ⁶He is not here, but is risen. Remember how he spake unto you when he was yet in Galilee, ⁷saying,

"The Son of man must be delivered into the hands of sinful men, and be crucified, and the third day rise again."' ⁸And they remembered his words, ⁹and returned from the sepulchre, and told all these things unto the eleven, and to all the rest. ¹⁰It was Mary Magdalene, and Joanna, and Mary the mother of James, and other women that were with them, which told these things unto the apostles. ¹¹And their words seemed to them as idle tales, and they believed them not. ¹²Then arose Peter, and ran unto the sepulchre, and stooping down, he beheld the linen clothes laid by themselves, and departed, wondering in himself at that which was come to pass.

¹³And, behold, two of them went that same day to a village called Emmaus, which was from Jerusalem about threescore furlongs. ¹⁴And they talked together of all these things which had happened. ¹⁵And it came to pass, that, while they communed together and reasoned, Jesus himself drew near, and went with them. ¹⁶But their eyes were holden that they should not know him. ¹⁷And he said unto them, 'What manner of communications are these that ye have one to another, as ye walk, and are sad?' ¹⁸And the one of them, whose name was Cleopas, answering said unto him, 'Art thou only a stranger in Jerusalem, and hast not known the things which are come to pass there in these days?' ¹⁹And he said unto them, 'What things?' And they said unto him, 'Concerning Jesus of Nazareth, which was a prophet mighty in deed and word before God and all the people; ²⁰and how the chief priests and our rulers delivered him to be condemned to death, and have crucified him. ²¹But we trusted that it had been he which should have redeemed Israel; and beside all this, today is the third day since these things were done. ²²Yea, and certain

women also of our company made us astonished, which were early at the sepulchre; ²³ and when they found not his body, they came, saying that they had also seen a vision of angels, which said that he was alive. ²⁴ And certain of them which were with us went to the sepulchre, and found it even so as the women had said; but him they saw not.' ²⁵ Then he said unto them, 'O fools, and slow of heart to believe all that the prophets have spoken. ²⁶ Ought not Christ to have suffered these things, and to enter into his glory?' ²⁷ And beginning at Moses and all the prophets, he expounded unto them in all the scriptures the things concerning himself. ²⁸ And they drew nigh unto the village, whither they went; and he made as though he would have gone further. ²⁹ But they constrained him, saying, 'Abide with us; for it is toward evening, and the day is far spent.' And he went in to tarry with them. ³⁰ And it came to pass, as he sat at meat with them, he took bread, and blessed it, and brake, and gave to them. ³¹ And their eyes were opened, and they knew him; and he vanished out of their sight. ³² And they said one to another, 'Did not our heart burn within us, while he talked with us by the way, and while he opened to us the scriptures?' ³³ And they rose up the same hour, and returned to Jerusalem, and found the eleven gathered together, and them that were with them, ³⁴ saying, 'The Lord is risen indeed, and hath appeared to Simon.' ³⁵ And they told what things were done in the way, and how he was known of them in breaking of bread.

³⁶ And as they thus spake, Jesus himself stood in the midst of them, and saith unto them, 'Peace be unto you.' ³⁷ But they were terrified and affrighted, and supposed that they had seen a spirit. ³⁸ And he said unto them, 'Why are ye troubled?

chapter 24:23

And why do thoughts arise in your hearts? 39 Behold my hands and my feet, that it is I myself: handle me, and see; for a spirit hath no flesh and bones, as ye see me have.' 40 And when he had thus spoken, he shewed them his hands and his feet. 41 And while they yet believed not for joy, and wondered, he said unto them, 'Have ye here any meat?' 42 And they gave him a piece of a broiled fish, and of an honeycomb. 43 And he took it, and did eat before them. 44 And he said unto them, 'These are the words which I spake unto you, while I was yet with you, that all things must be fulfilled, which were written in the law of Moses, and in the prophets, and in the psalms, concerning me.' 45 Then opened he their understanding, that they might understand the scriptures, 46 and said unto them, 'Thus it is written, and thus it behoved Christ to suffer, and to rise from the dead the third day; 47 and that repentance and remission of sins should be preached in his name among all nations, beginning at Jerusalem. 48 And ye are witnesses of these things.

49 'And, behold, I send the promise of my Father upon you; but tarry ye in the city of Jerusalem, until ye be endued with power from on high.'

50 And he led them out as far as to Bethany, and he lifted up his hands, and blessed them. 51 And it came to pass, while he blessed them, he was parted from them, and carried up into heaven. 52 And they worshipped him, and returned to Jerusalem with great joy; 53 and were continually in the temple, praising and blessing God. Amen.

titles in the series

genesis – *introduced by steven rose*
exodus – *introduced by david grossman*
job – *introduced by louis de bernières*
proverbs – *introduced by charles johnson*
ecclesiastes – *introduced by doris lessing*
song of solomon – *introduced by a s byatt*
matthew – *introduced by a n wilson*
mark – *introduced by nick cave*
luke – *introduced by richard holloway*
john – *introduced by blake morrison*
corinthians – *introduced by fay weldon*
revelation – *introduced by will self*